"We are used to thinking of horses as helpful, nobl
is less commonly considered is that they are also
wisdom. A horse will not judge those it encounters; it lives in the present, it
cares nothing for status; its thoughts are private and opaque – though one
senses the thinking nevertheless.

This helps to make the horse a remarkable animal in one respect in particular: they are – for us humans – supremely therapeutic. Observing and
connecting with these animals allows us to connect with parts of ourselves
which may have been neglected or unhelpfully split off. If you look at a
horse for five minutes, a tiny part of its tranquil and noble soul takes root
in you.

All this is especially true for those who struggle with language; those who
cannot easily connect the inside with the outside. In situations where the
standard 'talking cure' won't work, perhaps with children with autism, teenagers, soldiers with PTSD, prisoners, and others, connection with horses
provides a royal road into the unconscious – and to the rediscovery and articulation of disavowed parts of oneself. The genius of equine therapy is that
the horse at the centre of the therapy invites talk, but does not itself require
it to communicate.

This is a brilliant book for psychotherapists who may like horses but have
never yet considered the role they can play in their profession; and it's a book
for animal and horse lovers who knew that relationships with these creatures
were therapeutic but had never quite found the words to express it."

— *Alain de Botton, philosopher and author*

"The sections on working with alcohol dependent prisoners and bullying
contain practical information that equine therapists can use."

— *Temple Grandin, author, Animals in Translation*

"As a psychiatrist and psychotherapist I have seen first hand the power of
equine-assisted psychotherapy on the patients in my care. The field is still
poorly understood within wider mental health provision, and this book
helpfully addresses this gap. The author introduces the reader to differing
ways in which horses may be usefully involved in addressing problems of
communication, relationships, addiction, challenging behaviour and other
difficulties facing people presenting with mental health problems. I strongly
recommend this book to anyone working in mental health or with an interest in training in this field."

— *Dr Az Hakeem, Consultant Psychiatrist and*
Medical Psychotherapist

Equine-Assisted Psychotherapy and Coaching

Based on over a decade of sustained longitudinal research with a broad range of different user groups, *Equine-Assisted Psychotherapy and Coaching: An Evidence-Based Framework* is an essential guide which offers both theoretical foundations and practical models for working with horses in psychotherapy and coaching.

While not a panacea for distress and difficulties, the connections that humans find with horses can become a catalyst for deeper self-knowledge. By de-centring the human subject and placing the horse in the middle of the investigation, the ways in which humans make sense of themselves can be explored and more easily understood. Drawing on this wide spectrum of different client groups, the book features intervention studies with expelled teenagers, adults in addiction recovery programmes, children diagnosed on the autistic spectrum, people suffering from trauma and mental health problems, prisoners and even multi-national corporations wanting culture change. The practice of using horses in a psychological intervention is thoroughly scrutinised throughout, with ways of establishing successful change documented and assessed.

Liefooghe's analysis of these studies builds up to provide a comprehensive, evidence-based framework for equine-assisted psychotherapy and coaching. This essential book offers psychotherapists, coaches and all those who work in a helping capacity a clear insight into what horses can and cannot do in a therapeutic role.

Andreas Liefooghe, PhD, is Professor of Psychology and Leadership at Sasin, Chulalongkorn University, Bangkok, a psychologist at Birkbeck, University of London for the past two decades, and a psychotherapist in private practice. A life-long horseman, he founded Operation Centaur in 2005 with the aim of providing a sound theoretical and empirical base for the practice of using horses for therapeutic purposes.

Equine-Assisted Psychotherapy and Coaching

An Evidence-Based Framework

Andreas Liefooghe

Routledge
Taylor & Francis Group

LONDON AND NEW YORK

First published 2020
by Routledge
2 Park Square, Milton Park, Abingdon, Oxon OX14 4RN

and by Routledge
52 Vanderbilt Avenue, New York, NY 10017

Routledge is an imprint of the Taylor & Francis Group, an informa business

British Library Cataloguing-in-Publication Data
A catalogue record for this book is available from the British Library

Library of Congress Cataloging-in-Publication Data
Names: Liefooghe, Andreas, author.
Title: Equine-assisted psychotherapy and coaching : an evidence-based framework / Andreas Liefooghe.
Description: Milton Park, Abingdon, Oxon ; New York, NY : Routledge, 2020. | Includes bibliographical references.
Identifiers: LCCN 2019014466 (print) | LCCN 2019015330 (ebook) | ISBN 9780429319419 (Master eBook) | ISBN 9780367333461 (hardback) | ISBN 9780367333591 (pbk) | ISBN 9780429319419 (ebk)
Subjects: LCSH: Horses—Therapeutic use. | Horsemanship—Therapeutic use. | Psychotherapy. | Human-animal relationships. | Animal-assisted therapy.
Classification: LCC RC489.H67 (ebook) | LCC RC489.H67 L54 2020 (print) | DDC 616.89/16581—dc23
LC record available at https://lccn.loc.gov/2019014466

ISBN: 978-0-367-33346-1 (hbk)
ISBN: 978-0-367-33359-1 (pbk)
ISBN: 978-0-429-31941-9 (ebk)

Typeset in Times New Roman
by codeMantra

To the significant others in my life, human or otherwise, dead or alive.

Contents

Figures

On equine-assisted psychotherapy and coaching

An introduction

Being with animals has long been regarded as good for our well-being. Horsemen and -women across the globe will tell you that nothing quite clears the mind like a good canter in a favourite lane. Bringing animals into care homes, as we do frequently, gives a palpable sense of joy. It makes space for reminiscence and brings containment to those who don't experience much warmth and skin-to-skin contact. In the aftermath of 9/11, when many of the trauma specialists on site had failed, it was the rescue dogs that succeeded in helping the intervention teams to release some of the psychological burden they were shouldering. Animals help us connect with our emotions, and with the world around us, in powerful ways.

Horses in particular feature formidably in our collective imagination. The oft-mentioned Churchill musing *something about the outside of a horse is good for the inside of a man* still holds. Yet how we treat horses has changed dramatically over the last century. Just over a hundred years ago, they were still ubiquitous, working in our fields and in our cities until the combustion engine heralded their demise. World War One also signalled their end as a warhorse, and horse racing and sport are now the most common spaces where horses are to be found. That, and of course, leisure. Now they're back at work – in perhaps their most challenging task yet – to help us understand ourselves.

I am writing this book for two distinct audiences, although the readership will invariably overlap. There is a progressive trend to work with horses in a therapeutic way, and I wanted to offer an overview to those who work with horses of what actually happens when we talk of equine-assisted psychotherapy and coaching. From a distance, you could be mistaken into thinking that the only thing observed in an equine-assisted psychotherapy or coaching session is some people milling around with horses. Nothing could be farther from the truth. Like all experientially-based practices, you have to be in it to appreciate its significant learning. No-one would think anything was happening if they were to peer into my consulting rooms, either, other than two or more people sharing a space and talking. That horses belong to nature and language to culture is one of the central themes of this book, and I hope to convey that connecting the two is a potent vehicle for understanding.

To psychotherapists and coaches, I wanted to recount the amazing shifts in understanding in the process of their work when horses become involved. While I'm not here to proselytise and claim that everyone should now start leaving their consulting rooms and come and work in the fresh air, I hope there are some transferrable observations of note, particularly pertaining to the position of the therapist or coach.

Operation Centaur programmes

Operation Centaur is the name of the organisation I set up to promote the relevance of the working horse in urban communities, and this takes the form of heritage, conservation and community projects such as the maintenance of wildflower meadows, logging woodland and carriage driving. Increasingly, we have combined therapeutic elements in all the above activities. Developing relationships, training, horsemanship instruction, and caring for horses affects the people involved in a natural and positive manner. The benefits of work ethic, responsibility, assertiveness, communication and healthy relationships have long been recognised – and horses provide these benefits. Intimidating to many, horses are large and powerful. This creates a natural opportunity for some to overcome fear and develop confidence. Working alongside a horse, in spite of those fears, creates confidence and provides wonderful insight when dealing with other intimidating and challenging situations in life.

Like humans, horses are social animals with defined roles within their herds. They would rather be with their peers. They have distinct personalities, attitudes and moods; an approach that works with one horse won't necessarily work with another. At times, they seem stubborn and defiant. They like to have fun. In other words, horses provide vast opportunities for metaphorical learning, an effective technique when working with even the most challenging individuals or groups. Horses require us to work, whether in caring for them or working with them.

In an era when immediate gratification and the "easy way" are the norm, horses require people to be engaged in physical and mental work to be successful, a valuable lesson in all aspects of life. Most importantly, horses mirror the finesse of human body language, which makes them especially powerful messengers.

The Operation Centaur equine-assisted psychotherapy and coaching activities are organised into a number of different programmes, each with a specific focus, alongside a general clinic. I draw on evidence from these programmes throughout the book, and it might be helpful to have a short review of them here.

Real Horse Power was first developed as an anti-bullying intervention for schools. When the herd and group meet, there are continual learning opportunities regarding fear, trust, cooperation and competition. Each student has to find their space in the mixed human/equine herd. By working through a series of tasks, challenges and obstacles, participants observe a range of behaviours in the here and now and process them appropriately to arrive at non-confrontational solutions. More recently, we have adapted *Real Horse Power* beyond an anti-bullying programme to allow children who need some extra help to participate and learn.

Harness the Horses is a pioneering programme that helps offenders transition from prison to ordinary life. Before their release, it engages prisoners in meaningful conservation work with horses in London's Royal Parks. As the programme has developed, we now offer spaces for anyone who needs assistance with transitions. A new partnership with the YMCA has already resulted in some significant changes beyond a prison or offender population.

As a result of the difficulties involved in getting prisoners out of prison to attend our stables, we explored getting our horses into prison instead. *Centaur Inside* is a rehabilitation programme structured into eight sessions over two weeks. The sessions run consecutively Monday to Thursday, followed by three days off and then the same pattern the following week. Each session starts outside in the prison yard where the participants meet and interact with the horses. One or more tasks are set and following completion, the group heads indoors into a private room for a group processing session. The whole experience takes two and a half hours; the split between the time spent with the horses and in the room varies depending on what emerges.

Centaur Recovery is our general admissions programme addressing any form of addiction and recovery therefrom. Treating addiction is a complex and comprehensive process involving multi-disciplinary programmes and modalities. Equine-assisted psychotherapy has been shown to be incredibly beneficial with this client group.

The Silent Language of Leaders has been with us from the beginning, and was first piloted in Bangkok during a residency I had there as a visiting professor at Sasin, Chulalongkorn University. Since then, myriads of organisations have participated and developed as a result. The philosophy of the programme holds that in our contemporary workplaces, we have lost (or forgotten) most of our survival instincts. Horses haven't. As prey animals, they rely on these instincts to stay safe and thrive. Horses don't lie, and don't tell white lies to make people feel better. They make accurate decisions. Watching our horses respond to signals individuals and teams give them offers an opportunity to learn in the moment like no other. It helps individuals to understand their places in the group, the roles they play, and the relationships they form. It invites each member to step up and take their authority. This learning gives organisations the opportunity to reflect on and to understand the change agenda they might need to implement.

Centaur Connections is both one of our earliest and latest programmes. It is an equine-assisted learning programme designed to overcome stigma and to address some of the difficulties in understanding others who are different.

Originally, we started this programme with teenagers diagnosed on the autistic spectrum. Latterly, we have broadened the programme to a fuller age range, and have included both non-neurotypical participants and those diagnosed with mental health problems. In the past few decades, many challenges around differences in organisations have been successfully addressed with regard to gender, race, age, sexuality or disability. Indeed, legal frameworks exist to protect discrimination at work of any kind, including during the recruitment process. Yet against this backdrop, there is still one large stigma remaining – that of mental health and non-neurotypicality at work. *Centaur Connections* seeks to redress this. Horses as radically different others are an essential methodology for this.

The Centaur Club is a space where young people can experience being with horses and others, and thereby learn about their own place in the world. The key aim of *The Centaur Club* is to undertake meaningful work with a purpose, where everyone can participate regardless of age and ability. The fact that the activities do have a wider impact is an important part of the philosophy behind *The Centaur Club*. Helping others and the environment is a great way to help yourself, too. In this respect, horses are incredible teachers. *The Centaur Club* offers an opportunity to engage in meaningful tasks that make a positive impact on the natural environment. It allows participants to be part of a healthy and fair work and learning environment, and to improve their psychological well-being. It allows us to offer a therapeutic intervention to hard-to-reach groups. Most of the participants in *The Centaur Club* have been children or young adults in foster care. Taking care of horses is therefore particularly poignant.

Our *General Programme* includes one-to-one, couple and group equine-assisted psychotherapy and coaching. This has included addressing issues of co-dependence, psychological and emotional issues such as depression, grief, anxiety, anger management and relational exigencies. We have also run successful bereavement groups.

In sum, we have worked with some of the most difficult to reach individuals and groups in society. Time and again, we have demonstrated that bringing our horses to the centre of the Operation Centaur experience, investigating how we connect, and through that connection exploring our relationships and roles, a vast opportunity to help understanding can be facilitated. By applying the Operation Centaur model carefully and judiciously, with a great team of professionals and super horses, it is satisfying to provide this corpus of evidence, and intertwine these empirical findings with theoretical grounding.

Confidentiality and anonymity

A note on confidentiality and anonymity is important: I have ensured that names of individuals and organisations are not mentioned throughout the manuscript.

In order to do so, some of the details of the organisation will have changed, such as the sector or industry they are operative in, for example. When discussing individual patients, cases presented are always composites, elements of different people forged together to illustrate general points of learning rather than adding idiosyncratic background details that are unique to a particular individual.

With the exception of Zoltan, our Arabian, and two deceased therapy horses called Jim and Philippa, I also preserve the anonymity of the therapy horses. This is for therapeutic reasons. Our horses present with their own subjectivity. The moment we add a name to this picture, we already limit the experience. If I tell a client a horse is called George, and their father is called George, and they don't have a particularly great relationship, this will transfer onto the relationship with the horse. It is also useful to ask people to name the horses. Some will give them names of relatives and friends because of some shared characteristics. Corporates have given some horses the names of their competitors, or an absent leader. In bereavement work, the horse frequently, and usually after an extended and often debilitating time, receives the name of the lost loved one. Naming can be very powerful indeed. Some people find this mean, and are challenged by this withholding – yet it is also an act of generosity, to provide as much learning for them as possible. It's a great place to start some proper work.

Evaluation

At Operation Centaur, we use what is referred to as fourth generation evaluation.

Fourth generation evaluation, as its name implies, is the successor model incorporating three earlier generations of evaluation models (objectives, description and judgment) and moving beyond them to include intensive stakeholder participation in determining both the course of the evaluation and, additionally, what actions should be taken on the results of the evaluation. Data collected are qualitative, on the whole, although we do use psychometrics for some interventions.

Fourth generation evaluation is a model of evaluation that focuses on documenting change beyond solely measuring results, hard or soft. It is iterative rather than linear. It has been used successfully to evaluate mentoring and therapeutic relationships, transitions and personal change. The framework describing the process and content of this evaluation system involves: identifying stakeholders; discussing examples of actual achievement; logging the experience; stakeholder reflections on outcomes throughout the process; noting shifts and patterns; and having a plus-one – an external person solely focused on the evaluation process. Evaluation is an essential part of the Operation Centaur culture.

This book

Chapter 1 introduces the reader to the historical context of the horse–human relationship. I discuss how Operation Centaur moved beyond the traditional forms of relating with horses through conservation and heritage to therapeutic work with communities, individuals and organisations. We chart the flow from the physiological to the psychological, and discuss the various ontological and epistemological stances that can be assumed in reviewing therapy and coaching. We look at the various dimensions of the horse–human relationship, with an emphasis on how the horse has moved from object to subject in these accounts, and how this has given rise to various approaches to understand the horse as a participant not only in training but in therapy, too. We end this chapter with reflections on the figure of the centaur, which offers a new synthesis to contemplate the horse–human relationship.

Chapter 2, *Real Horse Power*, is in many ways the engine of the book. Here, I introduce the main philosophical and theoretical concepts upon which the book is based. We address language as cure, and the shift from a Cartesian rational subject to a divided self. We then look at some tools of the trade: the transference and countertransference relationships; projection; and context. This culminates in the presentation of the Operation Centaur model, which forms the guiding structure for the rest of the book. The elements of observation and safety, connection and reconnection, movement and direction are explored in terms of their relevance to equine-assisted psychotherapy and coaching.

In Chapter 3, the methodology of deploying horses, we are offered three main things: a radically different perspective; an opportunity to connect and re-connect from this different perspective; and the (re)evaluation of the relationships and the roles we hold. Furthermore, and crucially, the human therapist or coach is allowed to sidestep the traditional space they usually occupy.

Chapters 4, 5 and 6 develop the themes outlined in the notion that the horse has a technological function in the therapy or coaching. *The Horse in the Centre*, Chapter 4 addresses the notion of the other, and its role in de-centring the human subject. Via anthropomorphism, we problematise and resynthesize observation as a method and a tool in equine-assisted psychotherapy and coaching. In a further turn, we also reflect on the effects of de-centring language and the speaking subject. Chapter 5 addresses interconnectivity, or how individuals do not make sense outside of a context. We investigate spaces, and how what is internal and external is not always easy to discern. We look at the ways in which we can connect beyond language, and discuss how organisations seek to connect through their work with our horses. In Chapter 6, we review our relationships and the roles we play in them. We investigate the nature of our relationship vis-à-vis authority, boundaries and task.

Throughout any of our programmes, the importance of work itself cannot be underestimated, and in Chapter 7 we explore how and why this is the case. We consider the functions of work, and how work is one of the core predictors of positive mental health. We show how our horses have been pivotal, through their collegiate relationships with humans, in increasing self-esteem, self-efficacy and increased motivation and commitment.

Finally, a coda of personal reflexivity completes the book.

Figure 1 Shire horses ready for therapy at their stables in Holly Lodge, Richmond Park.

Chapter 1

Operation Centaur

Operation Centaur is an organisation set up to promote the relevance of the working horse in urban sites. We do this through conservation and heritage work, and through community and therapeutic programmes. HRH The Prince of Wales, who has been supporting Operation Centaur's work, refers to both our traditional and non-traditional roles of working with horses in London's historic royal parks and palaces in the book *The Last Herd*:

> In a further extension of their role, Operation Centaur now deploys its Shires as co-therapists in equine-assisted psychotherapy and learning. Shires that log trees and mow hay are also helping schools deal with bullying, raising the self-esteem of women prisoners and teaching that strength lies in collaboration, while leadership potential resides in us all. Words cannot do justice to what people experience when they find themselves face to face with a huge horse that weighs over a ton.
> (HRH The Prince of Wales, in Stewart 2017, p. 5)

In these uniquely privileged spaces, we work with our horses in conservation, treading lightly in sensitive ecosystems that have survived for centuries surrounded by one of the largest cities in the world. We promote heritage activities and deliver outreach and community programmes. For the past decade, we have also provided equine-assisted psychotherapy and coaching to individuals, groups and organisations.

Therapeutic work undertaken with animals is not new. Riding for the Disabled have used horses for decades to help children and adults regain a sense of movement and quality of life. More recently, hippotherapy emerged as an intervention based on physiotherapy on horseback. The different movements of the horse mean the client has to adjust and adopt different postural responses. As such, the horse influences the client rather than the client controlling the horse. It synthesizes the human and the horse in a very physical way. Organisations such as the British Horse Society launch programmes to engage disaffected youth through stable management and close proximity to horses.

We have recently made a jump from the physiological relationship to the psychological. There is a limited yet burgeoning literature that casts the role and relationship we have with animals in a different light. The research that has been undertaken shows clear indications for the effectiveness of working with animals in a psychotherapeutic environment. For example, when working with children who had experienced violence in the home, Schultz, Remick-Barlow and Robbins (2007) found a significant impact on self-esteem and well-being after working for relatively short periods with horses in a psychotherapeutic context. A mixture of farm animals such as cows, sheep and horses have also been used in therapeutic programmes (Berget, Ekeberg and Braastad 2008) and have produced significant uplift in the self-efficacy and coping ability of participants.

Therapy and coaching with horses holds something unique, however. A flight animal of immense strength finds it within themselves to trust a predator, to allow them to touch their most vulnerable parts, to work with them – and then to seek psychic reparation. It could be done with rabbits, but it may lose some of its impact! Horses respond with unique insight into exactly who we are in the moment. Their very survival depends on reading us right. So by reading their reactions to us, we can get a profound insight into our selves.

Centaurs

Chiron is perhaps the most famous centaur of antiquity, not in the least because he was the mentor (therapist?) of one of the greatest war heroes, Achilles. Centaurs in mythology were boorish and blunt. Chiron was the eldest and wisest of the Centaurs, a Thessalian tribe of half-horse men. Unlike his brethren Chiron was an immortal son of the Titan Kronos and a half-brother of Zeus. When Kronos' tryst with the nymph Philyra was interrupted by Rhea, he transformed himself into a horse to escape notice and the result was this two-formed son.

The centaur has always been the very epitome of energy, the wild child of the mythological menagerie. Centaurs are a fusion between Apollo (truth, rationality, wisdom i.e., Superego) and Dionysius (human, sex drive, Id). Human wisdom and cunning combines with power and speed. There has been a renaissance in the image of the centaur recently. Harry Potter books and films first reintroduced the centaur to general consciousness followed by the yoghurt-eating centaurs of Muller light. In the former, centaurs were seen as shadowy figures inhabiting a forbidden forest; the latter were referenced for their "unbelievable" status – zero fat. In the shadows and beyond reach are topological spaces that we often encounter during psychotherapy. The other-wordliness of the centaur reminds us of that shadow of the other in us, too, as Jessica Benjamin (1998) might put it.

Raulff (2017) calls the relationship between humans and horses a centaurian pact – the closer the bond, the greater the energy. In a wide-ranging exploration of the horse–human relationship, Raulff documents how for centuries this relationship has been inter-dependent, and has shaped our environment. Landscapes were altered to grow oats and hay so horses could be fed in inner cities. The stories we tell, our heroes and our foes, all rely on equine companions. People and horses were comrades in fate.

This was the traditional synthesis of man and horse. Can we re-articulate centaur from a contemporary perspective? By holding two halves that contain both base and elevated elements, the figure of the centaur shows us that these things do not need to be split. As we shall see in Chapter 4, splitting the world into good and bad is a technique that we all tend to use to manage our anxiety. A world where the good cowboys wear white hats and the bad ones wear black ones may not be wholly true but its simplicity appeals.

Chiron is also a healer. Because he was accidentally wounded and despite his immortality, he bore great pain – so much so that he renounced his immortality and become mortal, so he could heal himself. Combine this with his role as teacher and mentor, Chiron as a centaur is a good description of what therapy or coaching with horses is about – avoiding splits, containing anxiety, creating opportunities for learning so some understanding or resolution can take place: Operation Centaur.

Some history

When you observe horses being kitted out in pink and purple rugs, with glitter on their hooves and treated as pets, you could be forgiven for forgetting that the partnership we have has been millennia in the making. Horses and humans have a shared history dating back some 6000 years. Kelekna (2009) shows that what sets the horses apart from all other animals is the speed *equus caballus* offers. Through an effective relationship with the horse, humans can move further, faster. The first deployment of the horse was for warfare and conquest, but that was not all. Through the increased mobility of society, different cultures became linked, and trade much further afield became possible. The exchange of ideas came to fruition for the first time far outside of the home culture. Technologies were shared, religion diffused and art and science imported and exported. So while horsepower was initially and perhaps foremost an instrument of war, it also greatly extended the scale and complexity of civilization. Indeed, the spread of different languages can be traced back to the early nomadic horse routes. The language spoken in a particular area is in large part due to our historic equine partnership.

What allowed this to happen is the extraordinary relationship between the world's brainiest biped and the world's fastest quadruped. From war, trade, agriculture and the industrial revolution, in around 1910 a major shift occurred in the status of the horse. A transport system totally reliant on horses shifted to one that solely consisted of combustion engines – in the space of a decade. Similar stories can be observed in cities worldwide. Indeed, we would never have had Little Hans' horse phobia, and the resulting learnings on transference, had he been born a decade later. So from living in a society where horses and all their paraphernalia (and excrement) were all around us, we find ourselves for the first time in six millennia further removed from the horse than we have ever been. Horses are now regarded as no longer "useful", relegated to the category "leisure". What, then, of our relationship with them?

Pockets of an earlier relationship survive to this day, however. In a seminal study of traditional horseback cultures, and more broadly the archaeological history between horses and humans, Olsen (2003) describes the traditional Kazakh nomads and their horses. This lifestyle is still maintained today in remote pockets in North-western China and Western Mongolia. The areas where Kazakhs traditionally live can be quite inhospitable, and indeed their ability to have expanded into these areas is, in part, because their lives are intimately entwined in a working and cultural relationship with the horse. It could also be argued that the horses' survival in this terrain was assisted from the tending by Kazakhs.

For these Kazakhs, horses also form an important part of marriage ceremonies and funerals. A Kazakh man is said to never part from his personal horse while both are alive. After a man dies, his personal riding horse is tethered to a mourning yurt, and its forelock and tail are trimmed. The deceased man's saddle is placed on the horse, his fur coat draped over it, the whip affixed, and hat put on backwards; it is driven past several mounted girls, wearing men's hats put on backwards. The widow follows behind the horse. Following the funeral, the horse is herded with the other horses for a year, and then slaughtered at a funerary feast held near the man's grave. Horse races are organised at the feast, so that the man may hear the thunder of hooves once more. The Kazakh, in life, death and the afterlife, defines the world by, and is defined by, the world of the horse.

The relationship

In the Upanishads, the human is seen through the metaphor of the horse–human relationship, with the self as the charioteer:

> Know the Self to be sitting in the chariot, the body to be the chariot, the intellect the charioteer, and the mind the reins. The senses they call the horses, the objects of the senses their roads. When he (the Highest Self) is in union with the body, the senses, and the mind, then wise people call him the Enjoyer. He who has no understanding and whose mind

(the reins) is never firmly held, his senses (horses) are unmanageable, like vicious horses of a charioteer. But he who has understanding and whose mind is always firmly held, his senses are under control, like good horses of a charioteer. He who has no understanding, who is unmindful and always impure, never reaches that place, but enters into the round of births.

(Müller 2000, p. 9)

Discourses such as this centuries-old cultural artefact point to the important of the horse in how we as humans make sense of ourselves. Domestication, the bringing into the home, in and of itself pinpoints that there is a unilateral start to the partnership. Yet, as Bradshaw (2011) references in *In Defence of Dogs*, perhaps there is some mutuality, or at least reciprocation, to this relationship. With canines, the lure of warmth around the recently discovered fire, and the cooking of food, became part of the quid pro quo in offering protection. The horse, it seems, was more generous. Indeed, it is precisely because the horse could (and can) overcome its very nature that the relationship persists: an animal of prey that trusts carnivores enough to allow itself to be harnessed in leather and chains, mounted and to work in partnership with them. Raulff (2017) refers to this as the central paradox at the heart of the horse–human relationship: even when mankind's goals run contrary to the nature of the horse, it still cooperates. And it's precisely the horse's instinct to run and flee that was so coveted by humans in the first place.

Unlike cats and dogs, horses are born wild. They need to be "broken" or "gentled", depending on the approach one takes. Xenophon's still-relevant manual *The Art of Horsemanship* details how to prepare a horse for a theatre of war. In this text, Xenophon provided language that is still current in contemporary society, not only in the field of horsemanship but in any work context. He called the training space the "manège", which then formed the root of management, probably from Italian maneggiare "to handle", especially "to control a horse", ultimately from Latin noun manus "hand".

Dressage riders seem at one with the horse, and craft an exquisite partnership. The art of classical riding is very much about the symphony and synthesis between horse and rider – a slight incline of the head, a shift of posture, a touch of a leg and the horse will respond. Carriage drivers know that their hands communicate with their horses' mouth through the reins. In these relationships, we are taking the flight instinct and through skill and patience on both sides forming a perfectly symbiotic relationship. The language for taking a horse from wild to cooperative has shifted from "breaking" to "starting" the horse into work. This work aspect becomes important in the relationship. In horses there is a wild, dangerous unpredictability lurking inside them. It has fascinated humans for centuries.

From object to subject

How do we start this relationship? In the past, techniques have ranged from subjugation to cooperation. Do we want a horse that follows a leader out of respect, or one that follows out of fear? The main difference between the traditional and "natural" methods is whether the relationship is based on force and compliance, or trust.

The traditional method, originating from the earliest days of domestication and usually the preserve of the military, involves "breaking" the flight instinct, and follows instructions from antiquity as specified in Xenophon's *The Art of Horsemanship* (Xenophon and Morgan 2006). This is usually done by tying a horse up in such a way that they are deprived of their freedom. Techniques involve hobbling, tying the horse up so that they cannot move, or using straps and draw reins. By depriving them of their flight instinct, horses eventually give up and become docile. Once that point is reached, a saddle is placed on them and they are ridden. Those that don't submit are deemed too dangerous to ride, and are discarded.

There was a new wave of horsemanship in the nineties that brought a fresh perspective to our relationships with horses. Following the success of acclaimed film *The Horse Whisperer* starring Robert Redford (1998), the notion of gentling horses rather than the more brutal breaking in of horses gave rise to a movement called natural horsemanship.

Monty Roberts wrote *The Man Who Listens to Horses* (1997), on the behest of HM The Queen, who wanted the gentler ways of natural horsemanship more widely understood and applied. Roberts' quest is getting people to understand the "language of Equus" (Roberts 1997), where horse psychology is fully understood and appreciated. Roberts' Join-Up International organisation is named after the core concept of his training method. Roberts believes that horses use a non-verbal language, which he terms "Equus" and that humans can use this language to communicate with horses.

Equally influential was Pat Parelli. The Parelli Program is a people-training programme focused on the study of horse behaviour and horsemanship skills. The program spans four savvys, or areas of development, through four distinct levels of skill improvement. Before Parelli, natural horsemanship was unknown except in the secret inner circles around Tom Dorrance and Ray Hunt, and it was known as "It". Pat's desire to spread this knowledge to the world rose up in him after his mentor Tom said with lament that "It" would never go anywhere. Now this knowledge has made a major impact on horse training world-wide.

Natural horsemanship has its detractors. Some argue there is nothing new, and that these techniques have been around for centuries; others claim that the application and release of pressure as used in the training is in effect using anxiety as a training method, and that this has questionable ethics. While these no doubt are valid points, moving from Xenophon to

Roberts et al. heralds an important shift nevertheless – it has moved the horse from object to subject.

Throughout antiquity and until recently, horses were viewed as objects, as possessions – not dissimilar to how women were viewed, in fact. There are of course some notable exceptions. Alexander the Great managed to ride the mighty Bucephalus because he could take the horse's perspective. He had a theory of the horse's mind that allowed him to deduce it was the shadow of the man on his back that made him scared and would therefore not tolerate being ridden. By turning the horse into the sun while mounting, Alexander alleviated his anxiety and approached the horse in a partnership. Further testament that Bucephalus was a subject to Alexander is that the latter named a city after him. We all know Ignatius, Caligula's horse, whom he purportedly made a consul, and Napoleon's Marengo. These horses occupy subject positions, yet are very much the exception. Most horses were objects, and treated as such. The shift that natural horsemanship identified and strengthened has placed the horse more in line as a colleague to humans, and this is very much how we see our horses at Operation Centaur. This intersubjectivity is also the bedrock of any helping intervention.

Understanding the horse–human relationship

How can we understand horses and our relationships with them? Do we view them scientifically, as most veterinarians, farriers and physiotherapists would – a series of biological and physiological systems? Do we see them as unknown quantities that need careful interpretation in order to make sense of them? Do we look upon them as socially-situated and politically-laden objects? Or as a series of narratives, of discourses – as postmodern philosophers would?

Paradigms are systems of thought, and they are crucial to understand if we want to scrutinise our understanding of ourselves, others and the world we live in. This is relevant because we create all meaning and explanation based on observation, and observation in and of itself can be rather problematic. While it is tempting to think we are rational and objective, competing paradigms offer a range of alternative explanations.

Let us look at the example of one of our horses stamping his foot in the field, surrounded by a group of executives. To some, this would be a reaction to get rid of flies. To others, the horse is about to charge and attack. A third group hadn't really felt it noteworthy. The reality is, we don't know and we can't know why that horse stamped his foot. Nor can we know why a horse moves and reacts in a particular way – we can only surmise; in other words, interpret. If you have been around horses a long time, the most plausible explanation could of course be the normative, scientific one – a fly, or an itch, hence a physiological reaction. Yet for one of the executives the reality of a pending attack was so real he jumped through a six-foot hawthorn fence.

So the first explanation, getting rid of flies, is based on a theory of horse behaviour when confronted with flying insects. The action of a fly causes a reaction in the horse, so absence/presence of insect indicates leg passivity/activity in the horse. Many people, sceptical of psychotherapy let alone psychotherapy with horses, will default to this type of explanation. Usually, they will preface it with "they're just doing xyz". In my world, however, nothing is "just" anything. There are always multiple layers, various meanings, contesting hypotheses.

Scientific and normative thinking permeates the dominant Western worldview. Not only that, it is also hierarchically the most powerful and influential thinking. Science provides evidence. It offers certainty, up to a point. It guides our thinking, and it validates or discards our ideas. Most people will only accept that something "works" if there is scientific evidence that "proves it works". In these respects, science is still very much the modus operandi of an enlightened world. It is an attempt to question strongly held belief systems and to rigorously question and test any claims that may not be based on the scientific method: observation leading to the formulation of hypotheses, followed by experimental testing, resulting in the acceptance or rejection of the hypothesis.

Once we know how to sift facts from fiction, the second concept that comes in is how to distinguish that which is normal (the norm) from that which is not. The medical model informs all of us about this – what our normal weight should be, the level of our blood pressure, the strength of our eyesight. We can all clearly understand these norms. Their function is to tell us whether we indeed are in the norm, or outside of it. A nifty model called the normal distribution curve can help us plot ourselves versus others, and in that way plot how normal (or how "average") we are. As Ian Hacking points out:

> The normal stands indifferently for what is typical...but also for what has been...and for what shall be...That is why the benign and sterile sounding word normal has become one of the most powerful ideological tools of the 20th Century.
>
> (Hacking 1990, p. 23)

What is normal or not is in essence a subjective decision. Science uses the device of the normal distribution curve to determine whether something is normal or not – mean plus or minus two standard deviations removed from it is abnormal, no longer considered average. Yet the big inferential leap here is that we extrapolate from test variables (say, the relationship between caffeine and performance) and then apply that to the whole human subject. This is exactly why this approach is called reductionist – it reduces the human subject to a set of variables, or a set of diagnostics on various aspects. We receive many young people with a range of diagnoses, and tend to un-diagnose more than confirming the original diagnosis. Many complex cultural and social variables are involved in diagnostics. Anyone dealing with relationships professionally will come across this division, the need at some point to make a distinction. How to decide whether someone is sufficiently different? In a normative mental health paradigm, the DSM-V is the ruling technology deployed to ascertain what is considered normal and what not. It does so by checking lists of behaviours or symptoms on a series of axes. While this of course can be useful, it nevertheless excludes an important element. That which makes the human subjective.

Both the scientific method and normativity are regarded as highly relevant to the way we understand the world – is this also the case for the understanding and practice of equine-assisted psychotherapy and coaching? On the one hand, there is (rightly) a strong drive to professionalise a very young therapy. On the other hand, a mainstream normative worldview might not be the best suited to understanding this therapeutic modality. There is still a distinct lack of theoretical understanding of the practices, and other than Eagala (Equine Assisted Growth and Learning Association), no homogeneous practice body to speak of. Perhaps polyvocality rather than attempting to homogenise and speak in one voice is more important at this stage.

In sum, the approach to understanding and explanation discussed here is arguably the most prevalent one in the Western and developing worlds. Its principles underpin modern medicine, cognitive behavioural therapy (CBT) and solution-focused short therapies, and GROW (goals, reality, options, way forward) model coaching, to name but a few. The assumption here is that the world is knowable in an objective way, and we know how to get the true knowledge about the world by applying a specific methodology.

So why should this be problematic? Chiefly, because the reigning supremacy of a reductionist approach to understanding the psychosocial may offer explanations, yet does not necessarily create further understanding. An approach such as psychoanalysis would treat with suspicion anything that pretends to solve something. Fundamentally knowing what the solution or right answer is, is a very subjective thing. In fact, it would be very unusual for the drive for a solution to come up with something that is relevant to the presenting problem. Instead, care is taken to unpack where people find themselves stuck, a process horses can help with considerably.

What is therapy?

The word "therapy" can mean a bewildering array of things, from the physical such as physiotherapist and massage therapist, through to the psychological. For the latter, distinctions between the different types of psychotherapy, psychology, counselling or coaching can create misunderstandings as to what processes and activities we are actually referring to, and what background qua skills, practice and theoretical orientation we imagine the therapist to have. In addition to this terminology, there is also the notion of what therapy is there for. What is normal and not normal is one of the biggest ideological discourses of the twenty-first century. Who should have therapy, and for what reason, and by whom is part of our popular discourses.

Distinctions between psychotherapy and coaching are also very tricky. While psychotherapy has now become closely regulated, coaching is still very much fragmented. Trainings leading allegedly to the same proficiency differ from a long weekend to multiple years, and professional coaching organisations appear at times to be expensive membership bodies, or pyramid selling opportunities, or both. I established the first postgraduate qualification in coaching at the University of London, and one of the first things I do on the course is investigate all aspects of helping relationships. We are the instrument. Our understanding limits or expands the opportunities of insight for those we work with. It is the subject of the helper, psychotherapist, counsellor or coach that determines what work is being done.

While it is often said that coaching looks forward and psychotherapy backward, this is not necessarily correct or useful. The sentiment expressed is that psychotherapy accesses past experiences and coaching looks at goal setting and attainment. As you read through this book, I hope it becomes abundantly clear that this is a false dichotomy.

In the field of equine-assisted psychotherapy and learning, things are not necessarily clearer. Getting young people to muck out stables and groom horses, or going for a ride, may be referred to colloquially as "therapeutic" but it is not psychotherapy – nor indeed coaching. Of course, the facilitated space can have an unconscious effect. Learning from experience, when facilitated well, can offer profound insights. It is however the notion of *processing* that determines what level the work is at. And it is this – what this processing means, and what it constitutes, that needs clear articulation. Most levels of processing would include listening and empathy, as in general these in and of themselves can lead to insight and self-awareness.

What processing means to us, is to facilitate the unconscious becoming conscious and working through any vicissitudes this may entail. We examine, as Lyotard (1979) would put it, *les petits recits* – the small accounts – as well as the larger discourses that are used by our clients. We separate these accounts into constituent parts, carefully exploring possible causes, factors, significations. We listen to that which may seem uncanny. We help our clients and patients articulate a more clearly understood version of themselves.

Equine-assisted psychotherapy strips away some of the layers of conventional therapeutic intervention. It allows a relationship between the horses and clients to become the focus of the sessions. They can choose to connect or to not connect. As the therapeutic team, we can then step back and observe this relationship unfolding. Most equine-assisted psychotherapy, learning and coaching tends to be anchored in a person-centred, normative approach to understanding the human psyche. In contrast, the Operation Centaur approach is based in a psychoanalytic frame, for a number of reasons.

Psychoanalysis emphasises the determining impact of developmental experiences in early childhood, whether positive or negative. Overwhelmed by the experiences and possibly traumas of early childhood, the infant may defend him or herself and repress emotions that are hard to bear. The formation of our sense of self, our personality if you wish, in those early years often serves as a blueprint for the rest of our adult lives. We are shaped by these experiences, for better or worse. At various times in our lives, we may want to reflect on what goes well and what doesn't seem to function in our interest. We may have observed patterns that don't serve us anymore, patterns that reflect discordance between misconceptions ingrained in childhood and the experience of adult life that significantly conflict with the demands of reality. Here, psychoanalysis can facilitate understanding through making some unconscious drivers conscious, and this can lead to the individual making some choices.

As far as organisational and group work goes, the psychoanalytic work of people like Winnicott (1973) and Bion (1961) allows us to understand and explore these systems. Corporate coaching with horses heightens people's awareness of their blind spots. Who takes the initiative? Do we use all the resources that we have available? Can we motivate a team to complete a task? Or is too much of our time spent competing with others at the detriment of focusing on the task? Equine-assisted coaching gets people to know themselves and others in a very immediate way; less talk and more action.

Suffering can take many forms, and at times, our distress can be intangible, or perhaps indescribable. Working with horses in a therapeutic process allows you to see deeper within yourself. Rather than providing a one size fits all explanation, we listen to you, observe our horses, and work through the issues to create understanding, and to create a space where what is hidden can emerge. Whatever the struggle, people usually know when the time is right to come and explore. We aim to provide clients with an opportunity for personal learning and emotional growth, which takes place through their own experiences with horses during a session, or sessions. By doing so successfully, aspects of a person become re-articulated in more adaptive ways. Horses are particularly useful with this approach.

Therapy, psychotherapy and coaching

Most models of equine-assisted psychotherapy and learning will use some form of person-centred approach, a humanistic take, and psychotherapy and counselling that place the human subject in the centre.

Coaching has become distinguished from therapy by an insistence on a future goal and performance orientation for "normal" people rather than the resolution of past difficult issues for those with "clinical" problems (Spinelli 2008). This simplistic view however has been challenged on the grounds that the proposed difference is both a misconception of what actually happens in therapy (the present and the future are often key concerns) and coaching (existential issues are frequently brought to the surface). Coaching models have also been criticised for not addressing the immediacy of the coach–coachee relationship and as a result coaches can be naïve to the salience of their presence in the relationship.

Coaching practice often relies on techniques such as the GROW model (Grant 2011) which do not take into account psychological mechanisms holding client behaviour in place (Sandler 2011). In the process of finding resolutions to issues presented by the client, coaching is however more intimately connected to organisations and organisational discourse and therefore in a position to address social and systemic factors in a client's world. Thus, coaching inhabits a space defined by fuzzy boundaries which – if coaching practice is to advance beyond simplistic change methodology – are liable to blur even further into the space occupied by therapeutic practice.

For coaching to be truly transformational the connection to social context and relations in a client's world needs to be explored in greater depth than normative problem solving and goal setting allow (Western 2012).

We haven't found the cognitive, normative approaches of CBT and GROW to be useful, and will elaborate on the reasons for this in the next chapter. Nor do we see the usefulness of placing the human at the centre, and indeed introduce horses to de-centre the human subject even further. This kind of approach may not lead to quick fixes or elegant solutions, but it does yield important understandings that can form the basis for real change – something that is very difficult, and often traumatic, to achieve.

Indeed, we don't see our task as fixing things. Most of the time patients, clients and organisations come to us because they are fixed already – fixed on an idea, fixed on a relationship, fixed on a strategy that simply doesn't work anymore. We believe that their stuckness needs to be understood and embraced, and that there are good reasons for them to be stuck in this way. Helping to remove symptoms is dangerous – who knows what darker issues lurk, to which the symptom was a solution? Instead, we help peel away layers and nurture the sense-making of any given situation. Most individuals and organisations know what to do when they walk away, as they have come up with a solution unique to them; and nothing to do with us.

This approach is informed by psychoanalytic views on the world and the human within it. It is an intra- and inter-psychic system of thought, which we will explore more fully in the following chapter. In its current, intersubjective guise, it is an ideal modality from which to understand the horse–human relationship in equine-assisted psychotherapy and coaching.

Models of equine-assisted psychotherapy

No doubt influenced by the new wave of natural horse-thinking in California, the idea of deploying horses in a therapeutic capacity began in earnest. While there are many splinter organisations and the exact origins are disputed, the organisation called Equine Assisted Growth and Learning Association (Eagala) is the dominant world leader in regulating the practice and providing training. Formulated by Lynn Thomas, the Eagala model is a solid, safe and theory-neutral model of equine-assisted work. By way of comparison, I will juxtapose this way of working with another influential programme, Epona, established by Linda Kohanov.

Eagala proposes a fully-developed, professionally endorsed treatment model for mental health professionals practicing equine-assisted psycho-therapy. Unique to the model are the standards, code of ethics, continuing education requirements, replicable framework and team approach. Under the Eagala model, both a registered, credentialed mental health professional and a certified equine specialist work together collaboratively at all times to assure clients get the therapeutic attention and support they need as they make life changes.

The Eagala model involves no riding, making it both safe and effective. Clients work directly with horses; face-to-face on the same footing. This ground level work enables clients to better perceive the horses' actions and reactions as they work to process and solve their life challenges. Under the trained eye of the Eagala Treatment Team, horses offer clients honest feed-back and usable information that helps them understand how their process and actions affect others and impact their lives.

Eagala work with a partnership model: a horse expert and a mental health expert. The task of this pairing is to observe what Eagala calls SPUDS (shifts, patterns, uniqueness, discrepancies, my stuff) to document par-ticular aspects of client and horse interaction. These findings are shared with the mental health professional, who reviews the SPUDS observations and utilises them to help the client extrapolate metaphoric associations of therapeutic value from the interaction with the horse. This leads us to an important point of difference in how we work at Operation Centaur.

According to Eagala's research, equine-assisted work often helps clients change and grow more effectively and quickly than traditional clinical and psycho-educational approaches. They hold the view that an experiential approach is the most effective, where people typically learn best by doing. They assert that insights are more profound when individuals both under-stand them in their heads and experience them in their bodies. Working with horses, since it engages us here and now, is immediate and fully felt.

Where our approach perhaps differs the most is on the Eagala-held view on being solution-oriented. Eagala argues that their work is built on the premise that it's the clients who best determine the kinds of life changes they need to make in order to improve their lives. The job of the Eagala treatment team is to put the Eagala model to work to meet the clients' goals by engaging the unique intuitive power of horses to help them understand their process and practice the changes they want to make in a safe, supportive setting. Working to solve vs working to understand are two very different things. Eagala, then, positions the horse as an animal, observation of which can give rise to a number of metaphorical accounts – and these accounts, if enacted, can lead to insight and solution.

A very different position is suggested in Linda Kohanov's model of equine-assisted therapy, Epona. The Epona model positions the horse as teacher. More specifically, it positions the horse as having wisdom from a different place, one that we need to experience if we are to understand and change ourselves. In her two books *The Tao of Equus* (2001) and *Riding Between the Worlds* (Kahonov 2003) she positions the horse as a master empath, a teacher whom we should listen to in order to be healed.

The horse as mirror is a central theme. Kohanov expands on how horses have the ability to mirror us, yet not in the passive way most behaviourists would hold. Kohanov attributes intent to the horse; in other words, horses are teaching us deliberately to be better. In particular since the death of her foundation mare, Tabula Rasa (Latin for blank slate), she attributes to the mare, whom she sees as paradoxically embracing logic and mystery simultaneously, an imperative to explore.

> Rasa's lesson plan for me, and for thousands of people around the world who became her students in one way or another, involved a wildly expanded, inter-disciplinary approach to life. She insisted that we become more effective in navigating the challenges of a concrete, earthly reality, while also exercising our innate yet long-suppressed ability to collaborate with an ephemeral, eternally morphing spiritual reality, to claim our birthright as co-creators in a universe capable of dreaming big dreams. In this effort, Rasa taught us to not just appreciate mystery but to ride it, to use the challenges, frustrations, disappointments and pain of life to exercise a warrior's courage, not to conquer the known world, but to reach into the fertile darkness of the magnificent void and speak what has never been spoken, write what has never been written, paint what has never been seen, dream what has never been dreamed.
>
> (Kohanov 2011)

It would be easy to be dismissive of Kohanov's work, as a lot of it is rather shrouded in mystical accounts. She calls her sessions Black Horse Wisdom workshops. The central notion is that the horse enters and heals the participants. If we push the intent element of the horse, the horse's desire in effect, to one side it is nevertheless possible to explore a different account.

In psychoanalysis, there is the notion of *the person supposed to know*. What this means is that we all have a desire for knowledge to exist independent of us, especially knowledge about us. I remember vividly when I first started my own analysis how I really needed to believe that my analyst knew what was wrong with me, and what I needed to work on. Psychotherapy patients and coaching clients alike want to be diagnosed. It is this belief that the other knows that allows the transference relationship to be established as a working alliance. Yet the key task for the therapist or coach is of course never to believe that they do, in fact, know. They may have some knowledge and tools at their disposal (as we will discuss in the next two chapters), but they can never truly know what is going on for the other. That's the other's business – they need to become their own subject.

In Kohanov, we have the horse *supposed to know*. Whether the horse knows or not or can indeed communicate from the spirit world is a moot point, or even irrelevant – as long as the client believes that the horse knows, a transference relationship is established between the horse and the client that could indeed have a healing effect. Freud cured Dora from hysteria through the transference relationship, and Kohanov writes about a songwriter called Sanna who, disillusioned by the music industry, was creatively blocked. Kohanov describes how the black mare touches the girl, which results in the girl's ability to once more hear melody and write songs. Through the transference relationship, Sanna was able to express her desire and enjoy.

More problematic is Kohanov's position as mediator in this process, being urged by her horse to show leadership. Kohanov fears to be seen as crazy, and you can see that her fear is somehow well-founded. In *Civilization and its Discontents*, Freud (1930) refers to religion and spirituality as a desire to experience a sensation of eternity. He views this desire as a wish fulfilment, related to the child's egoistic need for protection: a powerful protection against loneliness and loss.

In conclusion, Eagala and Epona both offer some elements to inform any equine-assisted psychotherapy and coaching programme, although not always specifically as intended by their respective creators.

Figure 2 The Operation Centaur model of equine-assisted psychotherapy and coaching.

Chapter 2

Real Horse Power

Horses live in herds. They are social animals. These groups of horses offer protection, more than the mare–foal dyad alone can provide. Different horses have different roles in the herd. Rashid (2000) points out that identifying the alpha in the herd is simple – look for the horse that dominates, usually through fear and intimidation, and controls the other horses by biting, kicking and charging at them. Yet there are many other relationships observable, and different types of leadership. Rashid (2000) talks of horses exhibiting passive leadership skills, getting things done in the herd in a different way. Some may herd the youngsters and protect them; some exhibit prosocial behaviours, while others function as allies to the dominant alpha in the herd. Intriguingly, when a new horse joins a herd it is difficult to predict where in the hierarchy they will settle. Initially kept at the fringes of the herd, through demonstrating submissive and cooperative behaviours the new horse is gradually accepted. Their new role could be anything, and the old established roles could change dramatically, too.

People are born in groups, live in groups, work and socialise in them. Groups are a source of comfort and of anguish for us. As Bion (1961) points out, even when alone we carry our group with us. Our group helps us define ourselves by making us believe we have a role in the group, a role that is vital to the group's functioning. The groups we belong to help us create our values, our attitudes, our behaviours. In each group we are a member of (family, friends, work, gender, ethnicity), we are given the opportunity to learn about the expectations the group has about its members. This allows us to judge whether the cost of conforming to these expectations is worth the cost of membership. So thinking about ourselves in isolation makes no sense – in the same way that imagining a horse outside of its herd context makes no sense.

If we start bringing horses and humans together, we already have many things in common. We both seek comfort and security, we both need clarity around hierarchy. Where horses are perhaps more simple is in how they can live in the now. Horses don't bear grudges; they don't plot each other's downfall; they may experience unrequited love but they don't make their lives miserable for it. Relationships in horse herds are sorted, and the most important thing is the security of knowing their place. So while we have many gregarious elements in common, a key distinction we don't share is language. And while language, in effect, is the currency and the basis of most psychotherapy, counselling and coaching, when we do therapy with horses we will need to seek different modalities to work together.

This chapter is the "engine" of the book. Like most engines, it's both rather sleek and complex, in parts heavy, made up of different functional components, humming quietly but with a promise of fast acceleration – all essential to drive understanding. To be clear, the argument presented below is not intended to be a silver bullet. I am not promoting a new one-best-way of doing things. Rather, as you will see as you work through the various concepts, the whole point is not to offer a more precise answer, but a framework, or a stance, by which anyone can become more reflexive about their understanding of the horse–human relationship and the role this plays in equine-assisted psychotherapy and coaching. What we are seeking an answer to are the fundamental questions of what, why and how can humans learn about themselves through interacting with horses.

Power and energy

Horses have played a vital role in human development. Indeed, it's hard to fathom that the industrial revolution would have even taken place without the power of the horse. The London Transport Museum has a fascinating permanent exhibition on how horses were such an intrinsic part of the London streetscape. In a fascinating detail on one maquette depicting the development of the world's first underground train system, it shows pairs of Shire horses deployed to take the spoils away from the tunnels. Talk about making yourself redundant!

The power of the horse as a working animal is immortalised in the universally used measure of energy called horsepower, or hp. Engineer James Watt (hence horsepower eventually being called watts) coined the term in his quest to compare steam engine power with that of horses, the then ubiquitous power source. It is still an acceptable way to denote power today, with car engines being the most obvious example. My use of real horse power in this book is a metaphorical use of the term. There is a difference between the horse in the meadow grazing, and the word "horse" I use – one is real, the other symbolic.

"Horse" as a word belongs to the realm of culture – whereas the former horse clearly belonged in the realms of nature. This is an important distinction, as this becomes the basis for most therapeutic approaches; indeed, for most human–human communications. By making something metaphorical, we assume a level of sophistication, of understanding a meaning-making system: our language. While humans are born with the innate ability to acquire language, we do not arrive in this world pre-loaded with language and speech as such. This has to be learned, making language one of the most important cultural artefacts created by humankind.

The talking cure

Talking as a way of reducing neurosis to ordinary unhappiness first came to Freud (1895) as he became discontent with hypnosis as a way of rendering the unconscious conscious. Free association as the patient was supine on the couch would reveal repressed thoughts and feelings, and this examined life would allow them to make their own decisions and choices more freely and unfettered by past experiences. The notion of Freudian slips has entered our daily lexicon, and most people will accept that a slip of the tongue usually reveals a deeper thought one was engaged in.

We live in a therapy-literate, psychologised world. When Anna O first coined the term "talking cure", it was not so – talking as a way of accessing the unconscious in a dyad and finding through this an easing of symptoms was a radical intervention. Regular psychoanalysis on the couch is expensive, and out of reach for most, and most psychological interventions tend to focus on solution and cure rather than understanding. Add to this that many people who could benefit from therapy simply fail to engage with the process. What do you do if people don't want to talk, or can't talk?

The talking cure relies on language and on being able to express your internal world through words. In the various equine-assisted psychotherapy and coaching programmes I have run, I've come across different obstacles to language. On the one hand, there are those who struggle with language itself, i.e. autism. On the other, there are those who have progressively internalised the language of psychology and psychotherapy to the point that the signified and the signifier no longer relate at all. For example, we've worked with school-age children who will talk of "containment", "safe space" and their "feelings" without really connecting to what is behind the words. And finally, there is also a third group who refuses to engage in talking therapy at all, either through trauma or by simply not wanting to talk to a shrink.

Therapy is not solely reliant on language however. Bringing the horses as a methodology – in essence, a different form of communication – allows people to experience an emotional connection to another being without language. This can lead to catharsis and a lot of useful insights. When you whisper your secrets to a horse, there is a new level of non-threatening connection which participants may have not been aware of before. Animals fulfil a very important function in therapy and in establishing emotional connections. If nothing else, just being in the presence of another animal, elicits responses such as: "Being with the horse in the field made me feel connected." "It was amazing to see the horse walking towards me." "I felt like I was a happy child again."

The divided self

Are we experts on our selves? In the 1950s, the answer would be a resounding "yes". This was the era of the self, of self-help and to a certain extent a suspicion of those professionals "in the know" who were not to be trusted. The "self" became a personal project – I know where it hurts, I am the one experiencing this, therefore I am ... the expert on my self. To a large extent, this Cartesian view of the self still rules supreme in most therapeutic or coaching approaches.

Freud's (1900) most enduring contribution to Western thought was his theory of the unconscious mind. During the nineteenth century, the dominant trend in Western thought was positivism, which subscribed to the belief that people could ascertain real knowledge concerning themselves and their environment and judiciously exercise control over both. This notion of the human-as-scientist in a white laboratory coat who dispassionately and objectively dissects the world and sees it for what it is, is problematic. Is this really how we experience things? Sure, under exacting laboratory conditions it is possible to observe interactions between test variables. But let us remember in what context we are debating this – using horses in therapy. Any therapeutic intervention, no matter how much theoretical underpinning and claim to scientific evidence, is already quite a number of degrees removed from the exacting conditions that would necessitate any objective truth claims. Bring a horse into the mix and we very quickly have a rather contaminated laboratory! So what to do? Do we endeavour to remove error (= subjectivity) as much as possible? Or should we embrace the idiosyncratic, that what makes us subject, that what makes us uniquely different from the norm, that what makes us ourselves? It is my view that we should embrace the subjectivity and not be taken hostage by a world that is normality and objectivity obsessed, if our aim is to understand.

Unlike cognitive behavioural therapy (CBT) and person-centred counselling and GROW inspired models of coaching, psychoanalysis doesn't hold the view that self-knowledge comes from the rational self *per se*. We are not in the best position to know about ourselves, so the idea of self-help and self-reflection being able to help us come up with an answer if only we dig deep enough is fallacious. Psychoanalysis tells us how we are blind to what is going on for us. It is the process of creating understanding that can allow us to consider choices. It brings us to a freer place where we can make unfettered choices. A lot of contemporary approaches skip the "creating understanding" part of the process. They focus on quick fixes, moving from symptom to removal of symptom in the shortest amount of time. What caused the symptom in the first place is rarely addressed, therefore eventually the symptoms reappear in their old familiar forms, or in new and unexpected ways. So if we move away from the dominant Cartesian rationality, what can we put in its place?

In the *Phaedrus*, Plato uses a metaphor in which the self is a chariot, and the calm, rational part of the mind holds the reins. Plato's charioteer had to control two horses:

> The horse that is on the right, or nobler, side is upright in frame and well jointed, with a high neck and a regal nose . . . he is a lover of honour with modesty and self-control; companion to true glory, he needs no whip, and is guided by verbal commands alone. The other horse is a crooked great jumble of limbs . . . companion to wild boasts and indecency, he is shaggy around the ears – deaf as a post – and just barely yields to horse-whip and goad combined.
>
> (Plato, Cooper and Hutchinson [Trans] 1997, 253d–253e)

For Plato, some of the emotions and passions are good (for example, the love of honour), and they help pull the self in the right direction, but others are bad (for example, the appetites and lusts). The goal of Platonic education was to help the charioteer gain perfect control over the two horses. It introduces the notion of a self divided.

The first Freudian topology theorised three main psychological spaces: conscious, preconscious and unconscious. As such, Freud (1899) gave the unconscious content, a repressive function that runs counter to Cartesian rationality. Through formulating the unconscious, Freud shows free will to be delusion, and that we are not completely aware of why and how we act, think or feel in a certain way. Freud (1900) developed his first topology of the psyche in *The Interpretation of Dreams* in which he proposed the argument that the unconscious exists and described a method for gaining access to it. The preconscious was described as a layer between conscious and unconscious thought – that which we could access with a little effort. Freud argues that understanding about ourselves is achieved through transforming and mastering the unconscious, rather than through denying or repressing it. Crucial to the operation of the unconscious is "repression". According to Freud, people often experience thoughts and feelings that are so painful that they cannot bear them. Such thoughts and feelings – and associated memories – could not, Freud argued, be banished from the mind, but could be banished from consciousness. The aim of treatment is to understand how they got repressed in the first instance, and to find a way to make them discussable.

The second Freudian topology (1923) consists of three parts that describe the activity and interaction of our mind. The model holds that the "id" is the set of uncoordinated instinctual trends; the "super-ego" plays the critical and moralising role; and the "ego" is the organised, realistic part that mediates between the desires of the id and the super-ego.

Freud helpfully uses an equine metaphor to elaborate:

> The functional importance of the ego is manifested in the fact that normally control over the approaches to motility devolves upon it. Thus in its relation to the id it is like a man on horseback, who has to hold in check the superior strength of the horse; with this difference, that the rider tries to do so with his own strength while the ego uses borrowed forces. The analogy may be carried a little further. Often a rider, if he is not to be parted from his horse, is obliged to guide it where it wants to go; so in the same way the ego is in the habit of transforming the id's will into action as if it were its own.
>
> (Freud 1923, p. 19)

We make this metaphor literal. If we are not the best judges of what is going on within us, then who is? We propose that careful observation and some time spent with a healthy and settled herd of horses will go a long way to help create insight into how individuals, groups and organisations function. Horses communicate under the surface. We all have this feeling when we walk into a meeting and we know that something has happened; there's been a disagreement perhaps and we can pick up tension in the air. Or when a partner comes home from work and knows right away that something is wrong with their other half, but language has not yet made it explicit. Silences are not neutral; there are different types and we have grown to be able to pick up on all of this. Expressions like "you could cut the atmosphere with a knife" reflect something that we all feel on a regular basis. Even after we take language away, we are still left with a huge amount of information that, although we sometimes pick up on it, other times we have been conditioned to ignore.

Put another way, introducing horses into the dynamics of the therapy avoids a communication between the therapist ego and the client ego and allows the whole self to be at play. Many therapists conduct therapy from their (rational) ego and appeal to the rationality of the client's ego. This leads to changing schemas, for example, or identifying goals in coaching. This ego–ego relationship bears little or no result, because the underlying drive is not addressed. Having the horses there helps the therapist enormously because the therapist becomes de-centred. In other words, the horse becomes the therapist, and the recipient of all (or most) transferences and projections. It allows the therapist to be in touch with their whole self to the extent this is possible, and through reverie (see below) in touch with the self of the other, both conscious and unconscious parts.

If we bypass cognition, where do we get our information from? One of the ways to understand these phenomena are the transference and countertransference relationships. Another is through group dynamics and valency. The horses pick up and react to this energy in no uncertain terms. This gives us new data to work with in therapy. They become mirrors.

Transference

Addressing transference first: we continuously transfer our inner states to the people and things around us. We may like a certain individual because they remind us of a childhood friend; we can feel threatened by someone because they resemble someone from our past who treated us badly. In therapeutic or coaching sessions, this transference takes on an important role. Through observing what the client transfers in the here and now, we catch a glimpse of the symptoms they present. By looking more closely, we may begin to understand how that symptom was constructed in the first place.

This is the case because we are creatures of habit. Far from the popular notion that we all love change, and change is good, we are actually far more likely to keep repeating a pattern than to change it – and we find great comfort in that. If we see these patterns of repetition as symptoms, we could say that we are actually very attached to them. They serve an important function, primarily to keep our held beliefs about ourselves from challenge. Yet they were put in place as safety mechanisms when we were quite young, when we didn't have quite as sophisticated an understanding of the world as we do as adults. When we seek therapy or coaching, it is usually because these primitive defences have ceased to work for us. We don't want to experience another iteration of the same experience.

The transference relationship within the professional helping relationship is key to observing what is being repeated. As such, these repetitions can be observed, examined and understood. At no point is there a suggestion for change – that's entirely up to the client. From a therapeutic perspective, our task is to bring the client to insight. Remember ego–ego versus self–self? We want our client to become their own subject, not influenced by our ego. In this, the horses are a great help. From the very beginning, the client is directed to the horse. This allows the horse to, in effect, be the therapist. As such, a belief develops that the horse *knows*. This belief of another holding knowledge that can provide answers is a fundamental aspect of transference relationships developing. And indeed, realising that the other doesn't hold privileged knowledge and it's up to you, usually signals the end of successful treatment.

An example is as follows. Jean approaches me and asks why the horse is ignoring her. I tell her I don't know, and suggest she might want to approach the horse again, spend some time and find out. When Jean comes back, she tells me she now found out why. She is always too pushy, too hasty in relationships, never patient enough, always gets hurt. The horse told her. In this example, a solid foundation for exploring the transference relationship between Jean and the horse has been established. As the therapist, I can more clearly observe since the transference relationship is not primarily with me.

Klontz, Bivens, Leinart and Klontz (2007) suggest that the use of horses, in particular, provides a metaphor to elicit a range of emotions and behaviours in humans, which can be used as a catalyst for personal awareness and growth (Zugich, Klontz and Leinart 2002). Horses therefore offer a variety of opportunities for projection and transference. A horse walking away, ignoring, being distracted by other horses, sleeping, wanting to eat at the wrong time, biting, urinating and neighing are common horse behaviours that are reported as triggers for client responses in therapeutic situations. Clients can also often relate to a horse's natural hyper-vigilance and impulse to escape when the horse feels frightened or threatened (Burgon 2003). A client's interpretation of a horse's movements, behaviours and reactions determines the meaning of the metaphor and, as such, provides a relatively unique access point for unresolved issues.

Klontz et al. (2007) argue that by bringing forth transference reactions in the here-and-now of therapy, real progress can be made with clients. It is also argued that horses can give accurate and unbiased feedback, mirroring both the physical and emotional states of the participant during exercises and providing clients with an opportunity to raise their awareness. Zugich et al (2002) also suggest that this process allows clients to practice congruence between their feelings and behaviours. In addition, whereas it may be fairly easy to dismiss a transference reaction to a therapist or group member as a legitimate reaction to the target's short-comings or inappropriate actions, it is much more difficult to attribute a transference reaction to the shortcomings, inappropriate behaviours, or premeditated offences of a horse. As such, transference reactions in equine therapy can often be addressed without some of the confounding interpersonal factors present in more traditional therapies.

Countertransference

Having touched on the role of the horse and the therapist, we now turn to this in some more detail. Why do we seek a profession where we help others? While on the surface a noble pursuit, it is vital that anyone in a caring or mental health capacity examines their own thoughts and feelings that govern their choices. Altruism usually has a kick-back for the self, and there's nothing wrong with that. What would be wrong is to deny that this is the case.

Being aware of your own processes as a therapist is called countertransference. This refers to a therapist's unconscious reactions to the feelings projected onto them by the client. Transference of the patient thus influences the therapist's unconscious. Freud saw it as the analyst's responsibility to recognise and overcome countertransference to avoid it interfering with successful treatment.

In countertransference the analyst can assume that his own emotional response is based on a "correct" interpretation of the patient's true intentions or meaning (Rycroft 1995). The patient brings pressure to bear on the therapist to identify with his or her feelings and the analyst feels pressured into acting out a role, sometimes very subtly and sometimes with greater force (Rycroft 1995). The emotional response of the analyst to the patient was described by Heimann as "an instrument of research into the patient's unconscious" (Heimann 1950, p. 81).

In any therapeutic process, there may be periods of silence, times when there is a battle for the patient to find their words or a time when words tumble out in a stream of release. Whatever the tempo of the session the analyst needs to listen attentively. In listening the analyst should rid himself of any pre-conception, approximating to a state of pure naiveté, a state of "not knowing" in order to make room for insights that might illuminate a problem that excites curiosity (Bion 1965). He goes further to say that every session should begin without memory, without desire (Bion 1967). This state of naiveté is often known as reverie which Ogden (1997) describes in terms of ruminations, day dreams and fantasies and includes bodily sensations, fleeting perceptions, images and phrases that run through our minds:

> Reverie is an emotional compass, which I rely on heavily (but cannot clearly read) to gain my bearings in the analytic situation. The emotional tumult associated with reverie usually feels as if it is primarily, if not entirely, a reflection of the way in which one is not being an analyst at that moment. It is the dimension of our experience that most feels like a manifestation of our failure to be receptive, understanding, compassionate, observant, attentive, diligent, intelligent and so on. Instead, emotional disturbances associated with reverie feel like a product of our own interfering current preoccupations, excessive narcissistic self-absorption, immaturity, inexperience, fatigue, inadequate training, unresolved emotional conflicts etc.
>
> (Ogden 1997, p. 571)

What about the countertransference of the horse? Horses react to energy. Their countertransference is there for all to see, if you know where to look. By paying as much attention to the actions and reactions of the horse as to those of the client, we observe what goes on between the horses and the clients, while the therapist or therapy team remove themselves as much as possible from the picture. While it is often said that horses are "in the now", this is clearly not entirely true. Yes, horses tend to be quite often in a state of now-ness, yet that doesn't exclude the fact that they have histories, and memories. A fright at a particular place in the park will be remembered. A girth fastened too tight at too early a stage in the training may result in a life time of unease around girthing up. As with humans, possibilities of past experiences can be projected into the future, in such a way that a horse may become anxious when it is shown a saddle, for example. For both horses and humans, it is never the future we are scared of – it is always the past.

Projection

A particularly useful phenomenon to be observed in the transference is that of projection. This is usually observable in the first utterances people make about the horses. "That horse hates me," screams fourteen year old Sergio. Hatred is a difficult emotion to tolerate, and this young man struggles with it. It is easier to have something outside hate you rather than having to admit you feel strong hatred to significant others within your world. Alcoholics typically state that the horse "is only interested in getting its food, not at all interested in us", mirroring rather graphically their main preoccupation of getting the substance that sustains them at all cost, ignoring everything else. "It's like talking to a brick wall," said Tasha, who would not communicate with any teachers at school, "they're horrible ignoring me." When we asked Tasha whether she recognised herself, she visibly softened. "nobody cares how I feel, why should I make an effort?" By pointing out the projection onto the horses, she managed to take it back, and derive some insight from it.

Projection is a form of defence in which unwanted feelings are displaced onto another person, where they then appear as a threat from the external world. We do it because we cannot carry a particular feeling. It helps us keep the show on the road – until it becomes too dysfunctional.

Working in context

Winnicott (1957; 1971) was a paediatrician who later became a psychoanalyst and a child psychiatrist. He was able to integrate his knowledge of infants and his knowledge of the emotional life of babies and children, much of which was based on his work with war evacuees. His famous statement: "There is no such thing as a baby ..." (Winnicott 1949), meaning that a baby cannot be as a baby outside the orbit of the mother's care, cannot meaningfully exist outside a relationship, has enabled mothers to better understand what some might call symptoms as actually healthy expressions of the child's inner world, an attempt to communicate with its environment. It also brings the relationship to the fore in our understanding, rather than observing the internal world.

For our purposes, the existence of a holding environment in order to conduct our work is crucial. There is no horse without a herd or a field. We pay attention to the group and the context in which we operate. Many of our clients come to us to work in groups, whether the work is addressing bereavement, addiction, bullying or leadership. I love working in groups with the horses. It offers in my opinion the optimal setting for conducting this kind of work. People often learn more from watching others.

In equine-assisted psychotherapy and coaching, there is usually a task, whether it is the request to observe, or to comment on a specific behaviour, or to build a structure. In Bion's (1961) view, a work group is task-focused, efficient, able to get work done, and more or less in touch with reality. In contrast, the basic assumption groups (which I shall refer to as dysfunctional groups for easy reference) are focused on reacting to a collective phantasy – unconscious needs and desires that arise from the collective anxieties of the group – rather than focused on their task, which they approach inefficiently or not at all. So as the group struggles with task completion, these basic assumption behaviours surface.

The members of the group behave "as if" they were sharing the same tacit, unconscious assumption. Life in a dysfunctional group is oriented towards inner phantasy, not external reality. There are three different types of dysfunctional behaviour in a group. The first involves a group seeking to become dependent on one individual in order to feel protected and secure. The group members behave passively, and act as though the leader, by contrast, is omnipotent and omniscient. In therapy, someone might suggest something to do with the horses, only to be met by silence and everyone following the suggestion. Typically, resentment at being dependent may eventually lead the group members to "take down" the leader, and then search for a new leader to repeat the process. A second dysfunctional group is referred to as the fight–flight group. Here, the group behaves as though it has met to preserve itself at all costs, and that this can only be done by running away from someone or fighting someone or something. In fight, the group may be characterised by aggressiveness and hostility; in flight, the group may chit-chat, tell stories, arrive late or any other activities that serve to avoid addressing the task at hand. The leader for this sort of group is one who can mobilise the group for attack, or lead it in flight.

The final dysfunctional group uses the formation of a pair as its solution to deflect the task and to manage anxiety. Unconsciously, the group believes that only in the sexual pairing of two individuals will salvation be found. Usually, this expresses itself in two people, regardless the sex of either, carrying out the work of the group through their continued interaction. The remaining group members listen and are attentive, with a sense of relief and anticipation of a pending solution. Remember – all these dysfunctional groups are there for a reason: to get rid of the anxiety of the task, rather than focusing on completion of the task itself. I will elaborate on this when discussing our anti-bullying programme *Real Horse Power*.

Important for us, here, is that each member of a group is likely to assume one of these roles – saviour (or rescuer); pairing up; fight or flight leader. Because herds of horses function in this way, it is fascinating to observe the mixed human/horse herd in action. The stallion assumes the fight/flight function, usually as a strong pair bond with the alpha mare in the herd. The aptly named Trotter (1916) coined the term valency to look at this energy in a more streamlined way. Of particular interest to us, Trotter spends some time exploring notions of the herd. According to Trotter (1916), the interference of the human herd instinct makes us act in irrational ways contrary to what our ego would dictate us to do. He states:

> It is of cardinal importance to recognise that belief of affirmations sanctioned by the herd goes on however such affirmations may be opposed by evidence, that reason cannot enforce belief against herd suggestion, and finally that totally false opinions may appear to the holder of them as to possess all the characters of rationally verifiable truth.
>
> (Trotter 1916, p. 39)

In other words, we are influenced by others to do irrational things while believing ourselves that they are perfectly acceptable – such is the power of the group overriding the individual. As such, we don't find ourselves existing as individuals but as holding roles in groups, defined by and defining our contexts in the actions we take and follow. Herd behaviour or group mentality speaks to our desire to belong. It also appeals to our desire for certainty – we will gladly accept oversimplification if it reduces our anxiety, even if it's wrong. Important to our work, each person, unconsciously, has a valency to act in a particular way when requested to by the group. Just as the stallion will fight to keep the herd safe from rivals, the alpha mare will move the herd out of harm's way. Each horse as it is born will have a tendency to fall somewhere on the spectrum of leadership. Similarly, our innate make-up combined with our early experiences in life will make us particularly good at responding in particular ways to certain anxieties. Groups know this unconsciously, and mobilise the leader they feel will be the most successful at reducing anxiety.

Experiential learning

How do we apply all of this to the practice of equine-assisted psychotherapy and coaching?

Many people, when they first come to us, readily agree that they appear to live unreflecting lives and are content with simple answers to the questions surrounding experience. Seldom do we consider that much of our lives are not a logical thought-through process but one which is influenced by our emotions. Hopefully, by now, you are convinced otherwise. As Lionel Stapley puts it:

> Faced with any experience, the emotional learning that life has given us, such as the memory of a past disastrous relationship, sends signals that streamline our decision-making process by eliminating some options and highlighting others at the outset. In this way the emotions are involved in reasoning – as is the thinking brain.
>
> (Stapley 2006, p. 37)

It is when we begin to adopt a reflective approach that we frequently discover things are not what they appear to be. Through a process of exploring the beneath-the-surface dynamics of our everyday lives we can become aware of a different perspective. As human beings we can reflect on a past experience and picture ourselves as doing something, and we can then experience the feelings that we had when we were actually doing whatever it was. By self-reflection we can develop self-awareness that provides access to this world beneath the surface. Interaction with the horses facilitates this. We become not only aware of the rational processes, we also begin to understand the irrational, sometimes unconscious and emotional processes that are occurring beneath the surface; processes that are having such an important effect on our lives and on our organisations and societies.

While learning from experience is the hardest learning, it is nevertheless also the most rewarding.

The Operation Centaur model

I am conflicted about models. As a rule, I have always advised against using them. Models tend to make a practitioner lazy. It becomes easy to just follow someone else's thinking, so you prevent yourself from working at your best. Of course, they can offer guidance, a way to do things. More often than not, however, a model is given too much status. People attribute all kinds of explanatory power to models, whereas of course most models are how-to guides devoid of actual theory that could explain (not in the case of the Freudian ones quoted above, however).

So why am I proposing the Operation Centaur model of equine-assisted psychotherapy and coaching? In the first instance, because we have to build on the most prevalent model offered by Eagala. This model is an observational model called SPUDS, standing for shifts, patterns, unique behaviours, discrepancies and our own stuff. It points the practitioner to behavioural aspects of human–horse interactions using "clean" language (i.e., non-interpreted), while paying attention to one's own internal state. For example, you might observe that the horses start running when a certain individual enters the arena, or they change direction – shifts in their behaviour. You can observe that a horse in the session has twice walked from the gate to the watering trough and back (you don't interpret this as "thirst", for example) – a pattern. You may notice that a particular horse who normally doesn't approach people suddenly makes a beeline for a certain patient. People may describe themselves as very scared of horses and then place themselves by the back legs. As a therapist or coach, you may feel rather agitated/anxious/caring at an occurrence and use this as an additional observation.

I use this Eagala model as the basis for all the equine-assisted psychotherapy and coaching work I do. It is effective in its simplicity, highly professionalised and safe. The work happens on the ground, and there is no riding involved. While not explicitly stated, the Eagala model is very much rooted in the humanistic, person-centred tradition. It's experiential, with cornerstones of empathy, unconditional positive regard, congruency – and a commitment to finding a solution. My approach at Operation Centaur differs from this, for a number of reasons. In my experience staying at a purely descriptive level of pointing out behaviours as they happen can cause a lot of anxiety to participants. They may need something more from time to time, such as an interpretation. I'm also not particularly focused on finding solutions *per se*. I see my task as a psychotherapist or coach to facilitate a process of understanding. This increased understanding may then lead to the person making different choices, or decisions, or it may not. I'm fundamentally convinced that a "solution" is not something that should be forged in therapy, rather outside of it, in the person's own time. What I propose to add in my model looks at some aspects that are core to the human condition, and are shared with equines: the need to feel safe; the need to be connected to a group (or herd); the need or aspiration to have a purpose.

I challenge the reader to be critical of this formulation, however. The model is not set in stone. It is not necessarily fixed in a particular order. All it is here to do is provide a meaning-making framework that has served me well this last decade in helping me understand just how equine-assisted psychotherapy and coaching could work.

Safety

We live in a world where health and safety are meticulously addressed through the assessment of risk and the early prevention of hazards. Research has shown time and again that one of the main impacts to reduce mortality, for example, is not to address life-threatening situations *per se*, but rather to focus on the small breaches on safety that are made. Eliminate the small risks, and the safety culture this espouses will prevent greater harm.

While this sounds incredibly positive, it has its flip sides. I would argue that, progressively, individuals have outsourced responsibility for their own health and their safety to external agencies. "The council should check the cracks in the pavements so I don't trip"; "my company does the risk assessments". These legislative and practice frameworks have one downside, which is to remove the level of responsibility away from the individual. Someone else always makes sure I'm safe. It doesn't take too much inference to see this is a rather infantilising position.

Many people are therefore quite surprised when I tell them that I will not be responsible for their safety whilst they are working with the horses. We of course risk assess and select our horses carefully, but that is not really the point here. Ultimately, we are working with sentient beings, and I cannot presume that I or any member of my team can control these horses. They have their own agency, their own free will. Each and every one of us takes a risk the moment we occupy the same space with a flight animal.

This right from the start offers an incredible opportunity to address any notions of safety in the work. What makes us feel safe? What level or perception of risk regulates our behaviour? What risk can we tolerate? Physical and psychological safety are often intertwined.

I make it very clear that it is each individual's responsibility to ensure their own safety. I stress to participants that they should not ignore feelings of not being safe. If you're not feeling safe, you're not safe and you need to act on this information. You can decide not to enter the space where there are loose horses. You can jump over the fence, or climb a tree. I encourage people to come and stand behind me if they don't feel safe. This emphasis on safety, and the personal accountability it implies, is a fundamental aspect of the way we work at Operation Centaur. It strips various layers away, and in effect exposes us – it allows us to connect in quite a different way.

Connections

What happens when you meet someone on a blind date? How do you feel at the prospect of going to see your new boss? Or moving into shared student accommodation? An encounter with someone for the first time is a challenging process – and yet it is the fulcrum of the human condition. We are whom we meet. This connection is terribly important to understand, and usually, we do not have the opportunity to understand this as it is happening. We may be able to reflect on our anxieties, hopes and aspirations prior to the meeting, and indeed we can reflect post-event. During, however, is difficult. Working with horses in therapy allows us unique insights into this. How we connect, and what a connection conjures up can reveal significant aspects about the person.

The role we play in this as individuals becomes even clearer when the other is not a person, but a horse. Why do people choose certain horses and not others? How long do they spend with the horses? Why do we want to find out the anthropomorphic details of the horse, such as their name? Why does age or sex matter? We don't disclose any of this information, as we are interested in the projections. Some participants have been adamant that two of our geldings were mother and daughter, for example.

Reconnections

Once a connection has been made, following the processing of this, it is important to return and re-connect. This could take place in the same session, or the following session depending on the time available. To reconnect, either as an individual or as a group, can be a very different experience. Have things remained the same? What has been lost? What has been gained?

The connect–reconnect dynamic is making the strange familiar – and then, conversely, making the familiar strange again. It offers a real opportunity to work through attachment issues, and through loss.

Movement

Getting stuck is something many therapists and coaches struggle with. It is one of the most common questions when I supervise students, and it tends to paralyse us. What moves, and what impedes movement? Where do we get stuck? This part of the model is of particular importance to communications, and to appreciating difference. How can we avoid making assumptions that others understand us? How do we learn to take perspective? What is our theory of the other's mind? Difference clearly becomes an issue. How do we let someone who is not-us know what we want from them?

In groups, this is where cooperation and conflict first obviously come to the fore. The group is now more explicitly asked to complete a task of some degree of difficulty. Frustration at not knowing and not being told surfaces. Authority is challenged, resources ignored. How can the individual or the group stay focused on the task?

Movement also involves change and transition. From standing still to stepping forwards or backwards: speeding up or slowing down.

Direction

Direction is how we get sense of purpose. It offers a focus for our desires. What do I want? We may now have created movement, but do we have any agency to control it, to direct it? How do we impose our wishes on the other? Do we force or negotiate? How quickly do we give up? Where do we want to go in the first place?

Modus operandi

This model is designed to allow for as much transference as possible to take place, as many metaphors, for maximum learning. So how do we put it into practice? Each equine-assisted session will have some or all of these elements in them. It allows me to develop hypotheses and test these. Are we dealing with someone who is stuck? Or someone who struggles to connect? Is what needs addressing a lack of goals, or a fear that the world will not be the same following an absence? Each of these can be addressed by a different aspect of the OC model – the skill is deciding what to use, where.

To elicit this learning, I use a series of exercises. There is a lot of hype about these exercises – usually, it's the first thing interested practitioners ask. What do you actually do? I'm sure my answer is rather disappointing. In my view, it's never about the exercises but all about processing the learning.

So almost any exercise will do, as long as it facilitates an experiential learning opportunity.

Following the safety briefing, I almost always ask people to introduce themselves. Once we have processed this, I ask people to return and to reconnect, and to observe if things still feel the same, or whether they have changed. I then turn to movement, and direction. Endings are of course important, too, and I ensure that each session has some suitable time spent addressing the time frame.

In the next chapters, I will illustrate some of this work in much greater detail. We have devised situational exercises that allow very specific learning – for example, we developed the Cycle of Change exercise for corporate organisational development. Acres for Life, an amazing programme run by Lynne Moore for The Betty Ford Clinic (amongst others) guided us to exercises such as Temptation Ally, which we adapted for our use with drug addiction in prisons. At one level, you'd think there are only so many things you can do with horses in experiential learning. Yet ultimately, it is only one's imagination that is the limit.

Figure 3 "The Shireshank Redemption": horses entering prison for the *Centaur Inside* programme.

Chapter 3

Methodology

"The Shireshank Redemption: Storm as women lags get horses for 'therapy'".

This was the headline in The Sun newspaper for an article published in February 2016, shortly after the start of the first *Centaur Inside* recovery programme specifically designed for prisons. In no uncertain terms, the article suggested that the intervention was yet another example of "soft justice" and seen as a reward for the women's crimes rather than a punishment. An angry parent from a victim's group, bemoaned "being fed up of hearing stories of prisoners being treated like kings and queens while their victims are left with nothing". The article made clear that the project had been funded with private money but that it was not, in the paper's opinion, the best way to spend this money. The second half of the article was slightly kinder in tone, with a quote from us on the benefits of equine-assisted therapy and a closing statement from Andrew Brigden, Tory MP for North West Leicestershire and Chair of the Regulatory Reform Select Committee, who said: "We have to get these prisoners rehabilitated. It's about helping them serve their sentence and reducing the risk of reoffending".

The paper's position is understandable considering the little available literature on the effectiveness of EAP in drug recovery and the journalists having no idea of what actually happens to the participants in the programme. The sheer physicality of bringing two Shire horses into a prison makes for a great story. Add onto that our society's obsession with vilifying the poor and the addicted (with mainstream TV entertainment offering programmes like "Benefits Britain", "Can't Pay? We'll take it away!" and "Benefits Street") and it is easy to see the reason for the negative tone and grim outlook of the article.

Prisoners are some of the most disengaged people in our society. Prison has a poor record for reducing reoffending: 48 per cent of women leaving prison are re-convicted within one year. For women who have served more than eleven previous custodial sentences, the reoffending rate rises to 77 per cent. Ministry of Justice figures show us that during 2015/2016 the average cost per women prisoner was £42,776. Re-offending is costing the country between £9.3 and £11 billion a year; and we know that access to effective services such as drug rehabilitation play a major role in reducing re-offending. The landscape of addiction in prison is complicated: we have those that come into prison as a result of crime performed in support of their addiction who then continue to use while inside. We also have those who become addicts while in prison due to the prevalence of drugs, which is one of the biggest challenges for our prison service. Short sentences and "revolving door" prisoners, mean that new supply cycles of any kind of drug are constantly being established.

With such high stakes, it is necessary to look at other more creative ways of dealing with the problem of addiction in prison. When old methods don't work, perhaps interventions need rethinking. Imagine the following scenes. The metal gates clanged loudly behind us, followed by the sound of the double lock engaging. This was the seventh gate we walked through with our two horses walking behind us; their clip-clopping hoofs echoing through the empty yard. The grass, which a week earlier stood at waist height, looked as if it had been rudimentarily mowed down by a herd of hungry cattle. It never ceases to amaze me how quickly two shire horses can transform a landscape; both external and psychological. The sounds of the prison awakening continued, forever punctuated by the sound of closing doors. Loud voices protesting, yelling, bodies shuffling in the spurs, the guards' authority carried by their booming voices. We take the head collars off the horses and they head straight for the grass, resuming their mowing duties. They could really be anywhere else at this point and I envy them for it.

There is always just about enough time for a coffee before the women are released into the yard. You can feel their energy as they come in, one by one. Whatever drama they have experienced in their cell lingers for a little while; most of the time it's a perceived slight or the realisation that someone has been gossiping about them. Other times the guards are to blame, or the nurse, or there's a physical reaction to a new drug prescription. The outrage is very real and others in the group seem to show empathy and understanding. But as the session begins, the focus shifts to the here and now.

Every session of this two-week intervention starts in the same way: with grooming. As the women's confidence grows, so does the relationship between them and the horses. We go from statements such as "Horses are filthy; I'm covered in hair; why do we need to do this?" in the first couple of days, to "Oh look he likes it when I do this!" and "Do you think he knows me?" There is a risk of the women taking this process for granted, rather than acknowledging the part they are playing in building the relationship.

Having observed dozens of women go through the two weeks of intensive group psychotherapy which are the basis of *Centaur Inside*, we can genuinely assert that the programme is anything but "soft". Horses, however, may soften them up, allowing them to break down the internal prison walls that have held them back for most of their lives. Methodologically-speaking, that is why we have brought our horses into this prison.

Horses in their methodological sense bring a number of aspects. Following the various stages of our model, they function to allow us to reflect on safety, to facilitate connections, to allow an opportunity to move away from places we are stuck, and to experiment with new directions. Each of these allows for the construction of exercises to place the horse in a context. Horses in therapy are useful for dealing with people who can't or won't talk. Connections take place beyond language. Horses soften the participants, they take them out of themselves, they transform the prison space into something – paradoxically – far more containing.

Horses as method

Horses invite curiosity. With groups that are difficult to engage in talking therapies, the mere presence of a horse creates a buzz – whether positive or negative, it is difficult to ignore animals that size. Horses inhabit a layer of our imagination that is closer to our reality than we think. Most people are not neutral when we mention the horses. They will have childhood memories of riding and caring for horses, or negative associations of bad smells, kicks and bites. Even those who didn't get to work and play with horses will have formed an opinion through the numerous representations in popular culture of the long-standing man–horse relationship. The horse symbolises different things to different people, but it is also a subject with their own internal world, feelings and relationships. They exist separately from us, have their own mind, resist control – even though they can choose to cooperate.

We bring both the closeness and the separateness into the equine-assisted psychotherapy and coaching arena. We explain how horses react to human energy and how we can use this reaction to get a better understanding of ourselves and how we function in the world. They become what we want them to become, while remaining a different entity from ourselves. And it is this ability to mirror our behaviour from a radically different standpoint that can help us facilitate change in addicted populations. In prisons, horses allow us to accelerate the process of self-knowledge; time is paramount in a system that is both strapped for cash and needs to reach as many women serving sentences as possible in the shortest and most meaningful way.

Horses allow work at a psychological depth that speeds up the process and gets to the core of the matter. People struggling with addiction are a group that have been well documented to use language to avoid engaging with therapeutic interventions. More traditional talking therapies have been seen to have limited value because the addict subverts the treatment for their own purposes. Issues are discussed, but by and large stay at a cognitive level. Every addict knows that what they have to do is to stop drinking or using drugs, yet what becomes immediately observable is how all of them have a secret place where the determination to keep repeating the cycle is a treasured space and stays well beyond the bounds of the counsellor, therapist or recovery worker. This is why a lot of the helpers and recovery workers get very frustrated; they feel they get to a certain point with the addicts but can't get any further. It is at this point that the horses become a very useful methodology. To horses, the slogans have no resonance or meaning: "I'm going to prioritise my recovery", "This time I'm just going to focus on me". Horses are about walking the walk, not talking the talk.

It is very easy to be seduced into thinking that these are people who are taking their recovery from addiction seriously. But we observe again and again that these kind of statements just function as a defensive routine to get the helper off their back; their secret fantasy of being able to go back to the addiction is still there waiting for them like an old friend when they are released from prison. What we are trying to do is to get them to cut all ties with that "old friend", ask them to turn their back on this "safe, familiar and enjoyable space". It is not therefore surprising that the reaction to this is usually rage, disengagement or an inability to hear what is being said to them. It is very hard to ignore two shire horses. It's also very hard to fight them or to be indifferent to them. Whether we like it or not, horses forge a relationship with us, even if we are oblivious to it.

Method in therapy

Methodology, or methods, refers to the array of techniques, and sometimes tools, that are used in a therapeutic context in order to achieve the aims of the therapy. As such, there is (or should) always be a sound rationale to deploy a specific technological intervention. Otherwise, we find ourselves at risk of reducing therapy to its tools and techniques, which clearly it isn't. Below, I highlight a number of methods in psychotherapy that have been specifically useful to elicit understanding. I reflect on how these translate into the work with horses before I discuss some specific methods which utilise the horses for specific purposes in the therapeutic process. I'm using the *Centaur Inside* programme in particular to illustrate these methods as the groups we worked with were particularly challenging, and it shows the effects of the horses as methodology incredibly well.

The couch

The couch was one of the first technological tools in psychoanalysis. In fact, reclining without eye contact when recounting events in dyads was already present in ancient Greece. Contrary to popular belief, Freud introduced the couch not so much for the patient as for himself. He felt it a distraction to be looked at while reflecting on the processes of analysis. In *On Beginning the Treatment*, Freud states:

> Before I wind up these remarks on beginning analytic treatment, I must say a word about a certain ceremonial which concerns the position in which the treatment is carried out. I hold to the plan of getting the patient to lie on a sofa while I sit behind him out of his sight. This arrangement has a historical basis; it is the remnant of the hypnotic method out of which psycho-analysis was evolved. But it deserves to be maintained for many reasons. The rest is a personal motive, but one which others may share with me. I cannot put up with being stared at by other people for eight hours a day (or more).
>
> (Freud 1913, pp. 133–134)

It is quite possible that Freud's aversion to be being looked at was a fortuitous and monumental discovery. Freud may have adopted an approach that he took in part for his own comfort that benefited his patients even more. In not being looked at by the patient, the therapist may feel freer to restrain from responding to the patient from moment to moment and to turn his attention toward subjects and places within himself (Ross 1999). This approach may allow the patient deeper insight and emotional connection.

The couch as a technique influences my use of the horses as technology immensely. The horse also allows me not to be looked at, to reflect more profoundly, and to connect more deeply emotionally. The horse allows the person or people I'm working with an external focus to reflect and rest their eyes on. Arguably it is also this aspect of the technique that allows us to use the horse as a mirror.

The chair

Staying with furniture as technique, Fritz Perls' (1969) chairs allow us to look at the importance of moving and perspective taking in EAP. A central part of Gestalt technology, an empty chair is placed in front of the client. The task is for the client to imagine someone, whether themselves, someone else, or parts of themselves, in this chair and gesture or speak towards this "empty" chair that of course now is not quite so empty. From that position, the task is to respond to what you just said, from that different perspective, representing the different person, or part of yourself, or role. Typically, the client can move between the chairs a number of times to continue the dialogue. Using the empty chair technique helps bring people into the "here and now" of their present experiences. As they verbalise what's going on, the abstract becomes more concrete. As they take on the other person's role, they gain insight into their own perspective as well as that of the other. If the chair represents part of you or an internal conflict, you experience different aspects of yourself and gain insight into your struggle. This understanding in the here and now is the ultimate goal of the empty chair technique.

In equine-assisted psychotherapy and coaching, the horse becomes the chair. One of the ways we deploy this technique is by introducing new horses to the group. As someone wrote in their diary:

> A lot of people were bothered by the new horses. Some were angry, confused and upset especially because we weren't told and we got used to the old horses. In our lives we struggles with change and find it really unsettling.

We asked them what they thought the horses felt like, coming into this strange environment. They noted that the new horses were a lot more animated than the others. "We all realised they required less and much lighter grooming than the others. I realised that even though you may think you know what people may be like, the reality can be quite different," commented another. The different horses being brought in heralded a significant shift in the overall mood. They found difference hard, the loss of something they had cared for almost intolerable. "I found it hard putting my trust into the new horses after building a bond with the others"; "Change of horses was difficult. The fear of having to start all over again." Yet by processing and working through this with the other horses, a lot of valuable learning could take place: "It's actually not as bad as we thought," they finally agreed.

> A lot of the girls did not take too easy to the new horses. It did feel weird at first getting to know them quite quickly, but everyone adapted well. When I start my new job it will be weird meeting a new team but I will adapt quickly.

Changing perspectives, getting glimpses of yourself through reflections on the horses – could we have achieved the same outcome with the chair technique? In the cynical environment of a prison, there is great reluctance to make yourself vulnerable, and to be seen to expose yourself. Working with horses as a method achieves the same, but in a much less obtrusive way. Participants don't feel manipulated, they don't feel in a process – the connections they make, and the reflections they utter, are genuine and catch them unguarded.

Coffee tables, flower vases and carpets

A final technique I want to bring in here is to elaborate on the transference as discussed in the previous chapter. In a consulting room, many patients or clients can state things like "I really hate those flowers" or "that coffee table is just nasty". Coffee tables and flower vases here become transferential objects (Winnicott 1951) – it's easier to express your disgust at the colour of a carpet than to express it at your therapist or coach. Or even take the projection back and understand the feeling for what it is. Horses very often become these transferential objects, too – with the exception that they are also subjects, and therefore their subjectivity can be used to challenge the process of objectification.

Objectification is the process by which subjectivity is denied and a person or a group or an animal is treated as an object. In prison, for example, the gender of the horses became important. At some point, the horses became objectified as "men", and all the "male" attributes were attributed to them – they were careless, possibly violent, uncaring. "Man as object" is of course very different to "man as subject". As these horses developed positive attributes, such as nuzzling the women, respecting their space, allowing themselves to be guided, it was more difficult to maintain the horse/man as object. Through their subjectivity, valuable lessons were being learned: generalisation doesn't always work; we need to challenge the internal stories we hold; the world isn't black or white. As one woman put it:

> We all seemed to have a bit of frustration because we were not in control and the horses did not seem to want to do what we wanted them to do. Typical men! We didn't trust them at all, and they didn't want to be with us. Andreas and Raul kept supporting us, and we all kept at it and had patience. We all supported each other. Each solving the issue of moving the horse through the goal by giving each other a sense of belief made us believe in ourselves more. At the end of the session most of us felt more confident and had a sense of achievement. I learned that I shouldn't look at the world in a black or white way. The horses didn't hate us – we just hadn't figured out how to tell them what we wanted.

Territory, time and task method

Working with the horses in an experiential learning setting necessitates one of the most fundamental techniques, that of creating the frame in which learning takes place. So whenever we run a session, we take the boundary-giving of territory, time and task very seriously. The sessions are split into two parts, and absolute priority is given to the three Ts: time, territory and task (Lawrence 1979; Obholzer and Roberts 1994; Stapley 2003). It is important to have the buy-in of all participants, as this creates the boundary in which groups can perform a task productively.

Territory

We have two spaces: one experiential space which involves the horses outside in the prison yard, and one review and application space which happens inside in a common room with windows that look out onto the yard so that a visual connection to the horses remains. The prison yard is a stark environment; high fences, concrete walls, barbed wire and highly divided and boundaried spaces act as a constant reminder that this is a controlled environment with very specific spatial boundaries. The grass patches, unkempt and up to waist height when the horses first arrive, are progressively foraged by the horses as the programme develops. By the end of the intervention, we are left with a physical reminder that something – a change – has taken place. The horses have a very transformational effect on the space; what was an unkempt area becomes a wild flower meadow. They explore every corner of the yard and make it their own, either through foraging or by leaving their droppings. Crucially, the focus is no longer on the heavy locks, high walls and barbed wire; instead it is the very unusual visitor that demands the attention not only of the participants in the programme but also of the prison population at large. There is now a strange subject in the yard who strangely feels perfectly at home. The horse becomes the proverbial elephant in the room. Together with the therapy team, the prisoners and the compulsory attendance of a prison guard, the stage is now set.

The inside space is an old manager's office which has been adapted to accommodate groups. It's a small space with seating all around the edges. It has one window with bars on one side. In contrast to the outside space which allows some opportunities to wander off and separate from the group at times of pressure, the inside space provides an unrelenting scrutiny and the emphasis is more on processing and the application of the learning which took place with the horses outside into their own lives.

Sarah, who had chronic alcohol dependant issues, was adamant that once she was outside she could still have a couple of drinks while on holiday with her sister. Although she conceded that a few drinks tended to quickly escalate into uncontrolled violent binges, she was still arguing that her drinking was under control. Temptation Alley is an exercise with the horses that takes place on the penultimate day of the programme. Participants are asked to lead the horses through an alleyway full of apples and carrots. They are asked to specifically rename these food items with the things that they are struggling with. Thus, apples become crack cocaine and carrots become vodka and wine or whatever their "temptation" item is. Confidently, Sarah volunteered to go first and refused the offers of help from the group. She decided to attempt the task without a head collar and to lead the horse by gentle encouragement and subtle nudges. But the second the horse had a taste of a carrot in the alley, she lost control of the situation. The horse completely ignored her pleas to stop and proceeded to eat every single food item in the alley. Sarah quickly gave up and removed herself from the group and went to sit in a corner with her back against a metal fence.

It was through the processing group once we were in the inside space that she could put words to her experience. Struggling at first, she started to make the connection between her attempt at persuasion and that which came instinctively to the horse. The horse's reaction when presented with temptation was more honest and a true reflection of the way in which she actually behaved and a more accurate representation of who Sarah was. Sarah on holiday became the horse in the alley.

This is something we would see again and again. The horses' actions in the outside space, and their relationship with the women, would allow them to then draw clear parallels with their own life experience while in the more contained and reflective inside space. In a way, the outside versus inside use of space also mirrored their outer versus inner worlds.

Time

Time has a very specific meaning in the context of a prison. From the colloquial euphemism of "doing time" to the long hours spent inside the prison cell, attitudes to time in prison remain challenging. Prisoners' time is not their own. They depend on set schedules to be released and moved from one task to the next. In order to accommodate the *Centaur Inside* intervention, other highly prized appointments such as hairdressing or video links to court hearings need to be moved and managed by someone other than them. We had secured with prison authorities that *Centaur Inside* takes precedence over all other appointments that inmates may have, with the exception of anything to do with legal matters.

In reality, hair and dental appointments are really hard to get and thereby are the cause of a serious of dilemmas which the women face in their ambivalence towards the programme.

But the time boundary is an essential part of keeping the intervention safe for all.

The programme runs for eight days over two weeks. The first half is four consecutive days, Monday to Thursday, followed by three days of rest and four consecutive days again on the second week, also Monday to Thursday. The sessions last two hours: the first hour in the yard with the horses followed immediately by the second hour in the inside room. The time contract includes commitment to attending all of the sessions in their entirety. Leaving before the end of the session without a previously agreed reason with the group results in exclusion from the programme.

During the first session, we emphasise the importance of being on time and ending on time. A time boundary provides structure and safety to the therapeutic intervention. If nothing else, respecting the time boundary allows the client to see there are consequences to their actions.

Natasha was late for four of the sessions and each time she would have an excuse which involved blaming a third party. The fourth time she was late, after she had been warned that further lateness would mean she would be excluded from the programme, she asked to speak to the therapy team. She acknowledged that on this occasion the reason for her lateness had indeed been beyond her control. However, she had also realised that the other three occasions were, after all, her own fault. She further reflected that had she taken responsibility for her time keeping before, being late once due to circumstances outside her control would not have been a problem. The time boundary had therefore eventually allowed her to take her own authority. As she was serving a life sentence, the reality of time was a struggle for Natasha. She didn't value it but she was bound by it.

Task

In *Task* it's very clearly stated that our aim in bringing the horses into the prison is to help inmates to learn about and understand more fully their addiction. This doesn't mean that they all see it that way. As the headline in The Sun implied, some of the women do see this as a way to get out of their other duties, get favourable reviews for their parole boards or spend a couple of hours out in the sun with two horses and their friends.

In the first encounter, it is important to allow these various aspects to manifest themselves. The task through which learning about addiction takes place is very simply to connect and care for the horses. If at this stage we made the task too explicit, we may create disengagement from the whole process. After a few sessions with the horses, it becomes very empowering that emotional relationships start developing within the group and with the horses. It is at this point that the more explicit work starts. It is also at this point that some group members leave it.

From the first session, Cherry made it clear that she was not interested in horses. A horse stood on the side of her trainer as she constantly disregarded the safety briefing and the ongoing guidance from the therapy team. She tended to dominate the group and was a very vocal and confrontational participant during the first two sessions. By the third session, the task group started to take their projections back and exercised their authority. This showed up as a conflict between Cherry and some other members who were becoming organised as task leaders. When the therapy team reminded Cherry explicitly of what the task was and brought her attention to the environment she found herself in, she found the pressure too much to bear and exited the group. Her departure, as anything in Cherry's character was also very interesting: ten minutes before the end of the third session she decided to stick to a hair appointment she had booked instead of staying in the group. She was reminded that she needed to stay until the very end to continue in the group, but those last ten minutes allowed her to break free and thus avoided any deeper work which was proving too difficult for her to bear.

While it was of course a shame that Cherry could no longer stay, it provided very useful learning for the group. Processing Cherry's departure had got the group to see the horses' role in a very different way; this was not "pony club" but a mixed human horse group where the humans would have to work at a much deeper psychological level than they were used to or expecting. Cherry hadn't just been stood on by a horse; she was "trodden on" and the group started to see how it all related to being trodden on by life and the role that played in their addiction.

Outcomes as a result of the three Ts

Addicts don't like to be told what to do and that is part of the difficulty with conventional therapy and recovery interventions. Bringing the horses into the frame avoids "telling"; no language is needed as the experience speaks for itself. By then taking the experience inside we allow for processes to be examined and new learning takes place. Deploying horses as a technology to deliver addiction therapy avoids a lot of the pitfalls encountered by traditional therapy groups.

Experiential learning is the deepest type of learning and it is also the most challenging.

In a traditional group therapy setting, the therapist holds a specific place in the group. He or she becomes the object of projections, embodies authority, represents the wish to have an answer to things, becomes the "one who is supposed to know". For the therapy team to have horses amidst their ranks means that some of these projections and desires can be directed onto the horses. This frees the human therapist to be able to reflect and understand more quickly what is happening in the space. It is usually easier for the group to articulate vulnerable emotions towards a horse than it is towards a therapist.

Equine-assisted method

Within equine-assisted psychotherapy and coaching, there are a number of ways in which the horse can be positioned as a unique methodology. These include observations and the creation of a third party that doesn't speak and is radically different, something unlikely to happen in conventional therapies, even in groups. Having this additional presence allows for action – in other words, the talking therapy is not just about words but also about making these words concrete and thereby facilitating a different, experiential level of learning.

Facilitating observations and connections

Many participants used the contact with the horses to connect to both their own emotions and to their childhood. Although we talk about the here and now, what they are actually doing with the horses, their minds return to the past and make powerful connections. From a psychoanalytic perspective, addiction is typically regarded as a symptom; if we only look at addiction itself without looking at what the underlying cause is, our intervention will not be as helpful. The horses help our participants in bypassing addiction and returning to an earlier place. In prison and beyond, participants talk about not being judged, being able to "forget" about being an addict and realising they are more. This is perhaps what Kohanov (2011) calls "travelling between the worlds" but in an intrapsychic rather than spiritual way. The horses help them connect to their primal trauma, to that which gave rise to addiction as the eventual solution for it. The important question becomes: what is addiction the solution to? If addiction is the answer, what is the question? Horses become the methodology to connect, unobtrusively, without asking questions.

The return is also a reconnection with a more fundamental self, as opposed to the false self that we find in addiction. This takes us to the realm of narcissism. More often than not, under each addict we find a narcissist. Any attempt to deal with the addiction will not work unless we deal with the narcissist underneath it. The narcissistic injury results in the perception of a hollow core; you've created this grandiose self that stands opposite the tragic version of yourself around which everything collapses. You're hiding the fact that you are scared and you are going to somehow be found out. Many times we have seen how horses help release every narcissist from the burden of being special; they are not spectacularly successful but neither are they particularly tragic. Lack is also distinctly felt.

One of the women described this as a "pain that something is missing, like a gap that I can never fill". So while narcissism is the injury, how it manifests itself is very subject specific and can be seen in their choice of drug, for example.

The horses connect with the person behind the addict, not the false and grandiose self that we spoke about earlier. The horses don't see the women as addicts, or criminals, or victims. They connect with them at a more fundamental level. In the *Centaur Inside* programme, this is something that we observe during the first week. We cut through this false self and we get a feeling then for who is going to make it to the end of the two weeks. Those who don't accept the invitation to be different and connect with their former self, drop out. This process is not without pain, so the women are encouraged and supported. But there is one rule which is strictly enforced: if any of the women decide to leave before any of the sessions are finished, they are not allowed back into the programme. They are asked to prioritise their recovery before anything else and to make the right choices.

It is during this first week that the therapeutic frame comes under attack; authority itself is constantly attacked and questioned. There is a sense that unless the therapist is one of them, they don't have the right to question or acknowledge understanding. One of the women repeatedly and aggressively asked of the therapist "Are you a recovering addict? Are you? Are you?

If you're not like me, you cannot understand." While another decided very early on that the therapist was an alcoholic and held onto that theory until the end of the programme. It felt as if the therapist's alcoholism validated what he had to say. And it is this lack of acknowledgement of positive role models that shows how hopeless the mental space some of the women inhabit can be.

The challenge here is to be able to connect with them on some level with something deep inside you that can relate to their struggle. How does knowledge get categorised in the mind of the addict? We often encountered a debate between lived knowledge versus outsider (or expert) knowledge. This resulted in the person who needs help rejecting the help offered, on the basis that the epistemology and ontology they are given is not right since it does not relate to their own experience. Through this rejection, they can maintain their expert status. The addict says that to understand them, you have to *be* them. And if you are not, you will never understand them and therefore they reject your knowledge. The horse can disrupt this mechanism because it provides experiential knowledge but you get it yourself because it doesn't really come from a horse. This translates into a battle of authority: who knows more? Who has the *truth*? The addict needs to decentre themselves and allow the thought that something outside of themselves has more information than they do.

Building a physical representation

A further way to make a presenting issue more concrete is by getting participants to build the metaphor. So rather than just talking about having obstacles in our lives, we ask participants to physically recreate these obstacles, name them and then overcome them – while reflecting on what can be learned throughout that process. In prison, the participants tended to build an obstacle in the centre of the space, with all the materials we provide: cones, show jumping poles, and building blocks. Naming usually takes a while. What will this obstacle be called? What does it represent to individuals, and to the group as a whole? The construction can use any materials that are made available in their space. Sometimes, we ask them to use everything provided, other times we leave this option open – particularly if we feel the group hasn't used their resources sufficiently, and we want to create an opportunity to explore this.

Typically, with recovery groups, the first obstacle that is created is a massive big thing called "addiction" or "recovery". This is an obstacle that no horse could possibly jump over, not even at the Olympia puissance! It does, however, lead to useful processing, and obstacles get built and named in a less ambitious but achievable way. In particular, it allows for a discussion about goals, change and understanding, and the processes involved. Once an obstacle has been built, the task becomes progressively more difficult.

Initially, any or all resources can be used in the space. Then progressively, we make things more restrictive. We introduce a no-talking and no-touching rule, as well as no bribing of the horse. Before starting the exercise, the group also needs to choose a consequence in case they break a rule.

We process the task by asking a number of different questions. How you chose to build the obstacle? What does it represent to this group? Did you find it difficult? Easy? What was the process you used to problem solve this issue? What did you learn about yourself during this exercise? About each other? How do the behaviours exhibited during this exercise relate to the ones exhibited in your real life?

The obstacle task shows in detail the big differences between the groups that work well and the ones that don't. During this session, we present them with the notion of an obstacle but also of togetherness. And to understand togetherness they need to allow for the existence of "the other". If they are too narcissistic, this becomes impossible. The groups that work well together do not unravel; the others work with the illusion of togetherness and mention slogans such as "working as a team" but fail to do just that. Both outcomes provide enough data to be discussed with the women as examples of what happens when there is a good amount of support.

We also present the concept of impossibility: they believe at the start that the task that we set them is impossible. They proceed without any planning; they don't listen to each other or to the therapist. They are asked to create their own obstacle and in every group there is a tendency to make it too big and to call it big names like "addiction" and "freedom". This is in contrast with other therapy groups that are not drug users which will call the obstacle "first steps" and will create a more physically manageable obstacle. Ultimately, we are asking them to build a connection with someone outside of themselves. It is this request that is experienced as hopeless and impossible. They feel like they can't connect and therefore they won't connect.

As already mentioned above in the example with Sarah, Temptation Alley is another visual representation to help participants observe and learn from a metaphor made concrete. An alleyway is made in the paddock out of jumping poles, barrels and building blocks in an area that actually does look like a rather dangerous alley, with metal high fences topped with barbed wire. We place various tempting items throughout the course as distractions to the horses such as a food bin with chaff, fresh hay, carrots and apples. We then ask each participant in turn to lead a horse through the alley. Each participant is asked to label the various temptations/distractions that are placed in the alleyway with things that they struggle with within their addiction and recovery. For example, apples can represent heroin, carrots become crack pipes, hay can be an abusive partner. We then ask them: what labels did they place on the temptations? How well did the team communicate during this exercise? When you approached a temptation, how did you feel? What emotions did you experience? When did you notice there were other resources available to help you succeed in your task? Why or why did you not utilise the other group members/community to assist you? How will asking for help from your support system help you in your recovery? How does this behaviour mirror that in your using life versus your non-using life?

Remember, however, that these techniques and exercises are secondary to the actual learning. Equine-assisted psychotherapy and coaching cannot be reduced to a series of techniques. Charisse Rudolph (2015) has compiled a useful guide with various exercises and techniques for those wishing to pursue this.

Conclusions

So what are the results for the therapeutic process once we deploy horses within the therapy? Horses as a therapeutic methodology offer us three main things, beyond the use as a technology, technique or tool: a radically different perspective; an opportunity to connect and re-connect from this different perspective; the (re)evaluation of the relationships and the roles we hold. Furthermore, and crucially, it allows the human therapist or coach to sidestep the traditional space they usually occupy. The following three chapters explore this in further detail. First, we explore how horses allow us to de-centre. Second, we investigate how once de-centred, we remove the veil from our experiences and perceive how we are interconnected. Third, from this vantage point, we can examine and re-examine how we relate, and understand the roles we typically play.

Figure 4 Zoltan, as seen through the eyes of an eight-year-old girl diagnosed on the autistic spectrum.

Chapter 4

The horse in the centre

Natural history exhibits give us a fascinating insight into the minds of those tasked with organising the natural world. Once the programme of creating order through categorisation had begun, a complex process of vision and revision of nature continues until this day. Scientists would hold that these taxonomies are best practice, and necessary for our understanding of the natural world. I want to make some different observations here, and shift the focus to the human at the centre of the universe, the human who is making sense of it all. In other words, an observation of how nature and culture intertwine.

Historically, it was not unusual to exhibit animals that were deemed to be beneficial to us and those that were our enemies. In the eighteenth century, animals used for production typically found on farms were deemed good, such as sheep, cows and chickens; those that threatened this production such as wolves and rats deemed bad. A Friends and Foes exhibition at the Abegg-Stiftung in Switzerland in 2016 exhibited mediaeval tapestries featuring animals looked at the categorisation of animals to depict religion (the pelican, as it kills itself for its young, symbolising selfless love) and heraldry (swans, eagles, lions). As we have seen, horses have been universally depicted as positive, although descriptions such as "the dark horse" and the "night mare" give glimpses of a darker side. Good/bad or friend/foe categories are not always fixed, however.

Take the example of the bat. For centuries, the bat was classified with the birds and it wasn't until the seventeenth century that it was classified correctly as a mammal. Bats were symbols of the night, of death and of vanity, and therefore shunned and generally feared, cast as outsiders. Yet with the contemporary creation of Batman, the more benign characteristics of the bat began to be highlighted, such as annihilating vermin – now not only literally but figuratively. Contemporary natural history museum exhibits may sometimes juxtapose the "good" animal versus the "bad" human, however, giving the human a slightly different yet fully central stance in the classification system.

Observation

How the world is observed and classified is far from a neutral activity.

Observation is a cornerstone of many therapeutic interventions. Eagala, described in detail in Chapter 2, places the principles of noticing shifts, patterns, unique behaviours, discrepancies and our own sensory experiences at the core of their model. By describing things as they are seen using clean language, we get an objective view of the world. Examples of interpretation versus clean language would include *the horses are meeting each other* versus *horse a is walking towards point x and so is horse b*. The latter avoids the interpretation of "meeting", as this is already a subjective appraisal, perhaps even anthropomorphic.

However, is our representation of the natural world so objective? And is it possible to remove all human subjectivity? Should we, even? Most decisions are based on a particular, human view of the world. So while we view the natural history exhibit, we don't see the animal as such, rather the way in which exhibitors wish this animal to be viewed.

In order to understand animals around us, we need to de-centre the human subject. This means that we can no longer place the human at the centre of the universe and action our understanding from that place. We need to start looking at things awry.

We need to examine the subject/object split further in order to get more of a sense of this shift in perspective. What I mean by this is that the relationship between what is seen and what is being seen is mutually experienced, and that the idea of objective observation is – possibly – impossible. In observation, one affects the other, even if one or more parties do not acknowledge it (similar to the improbability that the scientist in the white laboratory coat could somehow be "outside" the experiment).

The "gaze" is the anxious state that someone experiences when they become aware that they can be viewed by another. The psychological effect, Lacan (1949) argues, is that the subject loses a degree of autonomy upon realising that he or she is a visible object, potentially being watched. This concept is bound with his theory of the mirror stage, in which a child encountering a mirror realises that he or she has an external appearance. Michel Foucault (1963) first used the term "medical gaze" in *The Birth of the Clinic* to explain the process of medical diagnosis, power dynamics between doctors and patients, and the hegemony of medical knowledge in society. He elaborated on the gaze to illustrate a particular dynamic in power relations and disciplinary mechanisms in his *Discipline and Punish*, such as surveillance and the function of related disciplinary mechanisms and self-regulation in a prison or school as an apparatus of power. The gaze is not something one has or uses; rather, it is the relationship into which someone enters. The gaze is integral to systems of power and ideas about knowledge.

Three main concepts that Foucault introduced are panopticism, power/knowledge, and biopower. These concepts all address self-regulation under systems of surveillance. This refers to how people modify their behaviour under the belief that they are constantly being watched even if they cannot directly see who or what is watching them. This possible surveillance, whether real or unreal, has self-regulating effects. In other words, the thought that they are being watched causes people to monitor – and possibly alter – their own behaviour. His formulation of the gaze entails that the human being's subjectivity is determined through a gaze which places the subject under observation, causing the subject to experience themselves as an object which is seen.

Why is this all relevant? Well, it shows that it is not just as simple as an observer observing the observed. It is an inherently subjective process, and any attempts to make it more objective – I would argue – function to deny in the encounter the partiality of the account. So any attempts to assume "clean language" when describing horse behaviour are in effect futile, as this denies our own subjectivity.

A poetic example describing the intrinsic impossibility of neutral, objective observation lies in the work of Alfred, Lord Tennyson. The Lady of Shalott must continually weave images on her loom to avoid looking out of her window towards Camelot; if she does, it is rumoured, a terrible curse will fall upon her. Instead, she looks into a mirror, which reflects the busy road and the people of Camelot that pass her by. The reflected images are described as "shadows of the world", a metaphor that makes clear that they are a poor substitute for seeing directly. After she has spent years avoiding looking directly at the world, "bold Sir Lancelot" rides by, drawing her gaze from the loom and the mirror to the knight in his finery. Seeing Lancelot, she stops weaving and looks out of her window toward Camelot, bringing about the curse.

> Out flew the web and floated wide-
> The mirror crack'd from side to side;
> "The curse is come upon me," cried
> The Lady of Shalott.
>
> (Tennyson 1842, p. 83)

The horse in equine assisted psychotherapy is the equivalent of the Lady of Shalott's mirror, in which people can see "shadows of the world" – projections of their own inner struggle. But the image that we've projected into the mirror must, at some point, be reclaimed. This process, of owning the once-unconscious currents of desire and pain within us, can be very difficult. However, it becomes necessary if we are to allow the horse to be a horse, separate from us: and if we are to gain the insight necessary to move to a position of understanding, and thence to a point where learning or change becomes possible. The curse here is knowledge. Once you know, you can never go back.

We see this in the story of Oedipus. The actual acts of patricide and incest in themselves weren't distressing to him; it was when he gained the knowledge of these terrible truths that his anguish fell upon him. It's also notable that everyone around Oedipus could see the truth of his transgressions before he could: we go to remarkable lengths to avoid self-knowledge. The horse allows us to approach insight and learning with an indirectness and a sense of personal agency that is difficult to match in alternative therapies where language is the medium of communication and the therapist is at the centre of the intervention.

Psychoanalytic observation

Psychoanalytic observation is based in particular in the work of Esther Bick (1964), and is formulated in order to establish a subject–subject dimension to observation. Its primary purpose was the training and development of the skills and sensibilities of psychotherapists dedicated to working with children (Rustin 2006). Observation offers insight into the psychic reality of individuals, groups, and institutions alike through a position of observation on the boundary – Benjamin's third position (see p. 37).

Particular attention is given to the context of the transference instituted between the mother and the observer, and between the mother and her baby. For an observer to enter an intimate space where mother and baby develop their relationship can be an intense experience where primitive emotions are evoked. Observing these experiences offers an exposure to vulnerability and powerful emotional pulls and provides a setting in which to consider the demands of a clinical encounter (Miller 2002). Bion (1970) talks of suspending memory, desire and understanding. This ability to float, clear but engaged, is an essential tool. These abilities include a need to be in the moment, to observe situations in the here and now and not in relation to previous encounters and to be able to put aside feelings towards the subject and abandon usual social convention. The process is not about building a relationship based on being liked for example, but rather a process to facilitate understanding and restore meaning (Kahn 2017). The observer also needs to avoid rushing in with fixes and solutions but rather stay with the discomfort of not knowing.

Moving from the clinical setting to a field of horses may bring its challenges, but it is not the first time that this technique has been used outside the clinic (Hinshelwood and Skogstad 2002). The method is inevitably implicated with the subjectivity of the observer themselves – this is indeed the point – the researcher's interpretation of events as a party positioned on the border of the organisation, inside yet not involved, gives them a unique position to observe and imbue the nuances of organisational life.

As Kahn (2017) points out, this methodology adopts the subject as an additional and central vehicle to elucidate the mystery of the observed system. It also presents the therapist with the challenge of examining the unconscious, "the psychoanalytic 'object of study' is, essentially, the unconscious mind" (Rustin 2006, p. 38). The challenge of observing, remaining alert and in tune, yet not immersed is significant.

As we discussed in Chapter 2, transference and counter-transference, the unconscious mental phenomena, are located in this process of observation. While observing the participants with the horses, the observer develops hypotheses following an examination of the unconscious mental phenomena observed during the period of observation. The therapist or coach watches and listens attentively whilst striving to not defend oneself against the feelings that are stirred up in oneself. Most groups will try to pull in those that are observing. A notable exception were the school groups, who very rarely inquired as to the presence of the observers. In psychoanalytic observation the connection between individuals in the group, their connection to figures of authority and leadership and to visitors to the group are scrutinised. The observer is examining individuals as part of a collective group. The observer considers actions are not isolated.

Observing the other

In our whole herd, we have only one jet black horse. It is very noticeable that this horse attracts more attention than the others – of course, it is a strikingly beautiful horse. Whenever she is part of a therapy herd, however, she has to carry more projections than any other horse. Often she is seen as male; most of the time as dangerous, as mysterious, or as mystical. I don't believe this is a coincidence. The way the horse is represented in our minds goes beyond our individual projections. In effect, there is a wider social and cultural representation of "the black horse" at work here, and this representation is not neutral. Significant meanings become attached, the black horse of this example becomes symbolic, it stands for something more than what she is in essence – a living, breathing creature of beauty. She also represents the other, that which we are not, in a very specific way.

Jonathan meets one of our Shire horses for the first time. The huge bay horse suffers from sweet itch, a condition that means he rubs his mane, gets sores and needs treatment. Jonathan is also covered in sores. They appeared when his wife divorced him and asked him to leave, which in turn lost him his job, and gave him suicidal ideation. The skin, as Freud (1923) holds, is a container. As the body's largest organ, the skin demarcates the outer surface of the self and is the part of a person most readily accessible to the observant eye. According to Sarti and Cossidente (1984), it is therefore the most appropriate site for the somatic transformation of subjective psychological contents. Throughout history various forms of skin reading have enjoyed popularity, from physiognomy to palmistry, and terms like "thick skin" and "thin skin" remain evocative. Some three months later, Jonathan no longer has sores. During his time on the *Harness the Horses* programme, he was mainly silent and difficult to read – or conversely, would speak rather manically regardless of whether anyone was listening. Yet we could see his demeanour was changing. When it became time for the programme to end, I asked him how he experienced his time with us. Jonathan told me that when he first observed the horse covered in sores, stoically enduring and being cared for, he recognised something. He felt that if the horse could cope, so could he. And that's exactly what he did. Through meeting a radical other, Jonathan managed to recognise himself. This is why in equine-assisted psychotherapy and coaching it is so fundamental to place the horse in the centre. By focusing on the other, we understand ourselves.

The other

The other can be a diverse and complex entity – an object of love and desire, a potential enemy and victim, a model for emulation and identification, an object of care and hospitality, a subject of his or her own destiny (Gabriel 2015). Horses present a radical alterity – we don't know how they think, feel, how they will react. It's also rather hard to find out if we are liked, appreciated, loved even – and indeed, if these things even matter. Meeting a horse is meeting ourselves through the other – as Martin Buber writes in *Between Man and Man*:

> What I experienced in touch with [this horse] was the Other, the immense otherness of the Other which, however, did not remain strange like the otherness of the ox and the ram, but rather let me draw near and touch it.
>
> (Buber 1947, p. 23)

We are born in what Freud (1923) calls a state of primary narcissism, a state where we hold that everything comes from the self and only from the self. In other words, there is initially no sense of another. An experiment called the rouge test, adapted from the mirror test that Gallup (1970) used to test self-recognition in animals, attempts to find out at what point a child has self-recognition. The test consists of placing a red dot, or rouge, on the child's nose and placing them in front of the mirror. Before a year or so, children don't realise the red dot is on their nose. Developmentally, this is usually a staggered process. At nine months, for example, there may be no recognition. In effect, the self in the mirror is still perceived as other. From 15 months onwards, there is more of a consistent recognition and the child does point to their own nose to wipe off the red dot. In other words, they have gained understanding that the reflection in the mirror is more than a familiar face; it is in fact their own. At this stage, they learn to distinguish between self and other, and learn they are different from other people and become aware that others may have beliefs, desires, and feelings that differ from their own. Initially, however, the child first encounters him/herself as an other and misrecognises himself as a subject, thereafter sustaining this recognition in the gaze of the other. This is in effect a first recognition that the unconscious is also the other within ourselves. In Freud (1923) in Chapter 2, we have already seen the other as part of ourselves, of course, through the super-ego.

Meeting the other

When a new board wasn't working together terribly well, we invited the executives for some work to our stables as part of a wider culture change programme. For this group (they are the leaders in their field, and a subsidiary of a vast multinational) we decided to deploy some Shire horses from our herd, in part because they, too, represented being the biggest workhorses in the world – and are rarer than pandas.

The preamble was a foreshadowing of things to come. Walking from the car park through woods, a transitional space, triggered various comments. "Where's the Starbucks?" people asked, giggling. "Who will do the emergency coffee runs?", the Human Resources team playfully (yet somewhat anxiously caring for their executives) wanted to know. Once in our hay barn, bales used for seating have been rearranged in an attempt to have a boardroom lay-out. When a groom appeared with a big teapot and placed it on the table, everyone waited to be served. Unfamiliar territory creates anxiety.

We asked the group to meet the herd, and once they had reached a level where they felt comfortable, to create movement. "Creating movement" as an exercise hits a number of important elements for organisations and individuals alike. We in effect ask for directed change, a move away from an impasse, a shift from the status quo. What are the methods in which to achieve this? What are the barriers? You can't just push a horse that weighs a ton! The immediate response was food.

"What do geese dream of? Of maize!" writes Freud (1900) in *The Interpretation of Dreams*, p. 132. Freud is quoting a Jewish proverb that alleges animals' and humans' dreams alike express desire, a wish fulfilled. Our desire, of course, already involves a different metamorphosis – it becomes the desire of the other. "What do you want from me so you will move?" ask our executives. The answer they suggest is "food". Yet food, in the form of some tufts of grass, did not move our horses. After all, they had plenty to help themselves to – the herd was standing in a field of lush spring grass, and they ignored the people who were hand-picking it and offering it to them. When grass didn't work, it was discarded quickly and carelessly. Longer grass from the side of the field was fetched. A horse farted and defecated, to much hilarity. Our equine specialist pointed out that the grass thrown on the sand could have consequences. Horses eating this discarded grass could swallow the soil, which doesn't digest and causes colic - in the worst cases it could even mean death. It was noted, but no attempt was made to pick things up. In the gaze of the other, participants felt very uncomfortable. What to do? How can we communicate what it is we want? In effect, very mundane and daily tasks in the working life of an executive. Yet here, facing these radical others, inertia took over.

On the perimeter, we had placed a number of tools: lead reins, head collars, and whips – aids typically used for equine communication. No-one had touched these. We asked why they had not sought to utilise these implements to create movement. To some in the group, they hadn't noticed. Others felt they didn't have permission. A plan was hatched to get apples, then discarded. We experienced the group as quite anxious, initially with the "bribe" being discarded, then giving up. These competent and very senior executives felt very lost when asked to create movement, and occupied a rather childlike and defeatist stance. They are tasked to change a multi-billion-pound industry, but feel they need our permission to use a simple tool.

So what is going on here? Relating to otherness is a crucial aspect of any organisational intervention, and bringing the horses into this embodies otherness in an undeniable way. The stranger-ness of the space and of the horses got people in touch with the strangeness within themselves. The gaze of the other made them take their sunglasses off. It wasn't that they were being observed; rather, they *felt* they were observed and had to perform in a particular way. This is why people usually want to connect with a horse through food – what do you want from me? If I give you food, you'll probably like me.

Anthropomorphism

Of course, one way of ignoring the other's difference is to make them the same as us. Science has typically rejected the notion that animals have subjective states. Anyone who works with or is around animals has seen that animals do experience emotions. Just as we cannot really ever confidently gauge the emotional state of another human being (with the exception, perhaps, of in the therapeutic setting), so too can we never for certain ascertain what an animal feels.

Our work in prison, for example, showed this very clearly. Working with a group struggling with addiction, initially all the group wanted to do was incessantly feed the horses. They felt the horses were lacking in things, and we were being cruel by denying them their sustenance. We were met with a barrage of aggression when we told them the horses were fed at regular meal times, and feeding them snacks in between just made them unsettled and discontented. Equally important were the tiniest scratches on the horses. In summer, most horses will get an insect bite, or will rub their tail somewhat, which results at times in tiny specks of blood being visible. The participants were incredibly concerned by these imperfections, wanting to tend to them straight away, asking us for creams and lotions. Most of the group of prisoners had much larger wounds and sores through intravenous drug use, but these were ignored. Finally, the horses were given a range of emotions – such as the horses had missed coming to the prison; the horses were having a row with each other; the horses were bored.

Horses may of course be experiencing all these things; we can't ever really know. What we do know, however, is that these are a range of human emotions that are attributed to the horses, and it seems very plausible that these emotions were experienced by our participants rather than the horses. In prison, it is difficult to say out loud that you miss something. It is the very act of anthropomorphising the horse that allows us to observe the human projection onto the horse. Seeing the other for what they are allows us to take the projections back; which grounds us as separate in the relationship; which in turn lends us choices.

The horse as pet belongs in this category. By being anthropomorphised the horse also becomes reified – an object for humans to project their desires and fears upon. By de-centring the human and placing the horse central, we can remove the veil of anthropomorphism and experience the relationship in a different way. Anthropomorphy needs to be seen both as metaphor and projection – we are shaping the lens through which we see the animal by our own experiences, usually by what we perceive to be desirable or not: in which case we are not seeing the animal as such. Anthropomorphy here acts as a veil – and it is by removing the veil (or breaking the mirror and bringing about the curse) and accepting the difference between self and other that much beneficial therapeutic work can be done. If he walks away, the horse may not be rejecting you, he may want to join the rest of the herd – let's understand what significance rejection by others has for you. It's about seeing the horses for what they are, not what we have imagined them to be in our initial experience.

There is one aspect of anthropomorphy that is very useful in psychotherapy and coaching, however, and it is one that allows us to see the horse as therapist. In Chapter 1 I concluded that Linda Kohanov was providing a useful insight into de-centring the therapist when she attributed almost-mystical therapeutic powers to the horse. Placing the horse as the therapist in effect allows the horse to occupy the centre. Jessica Benjamin (1998) talks of a thirdness. If the aim of the therapy is to make the unconscious conscious by recognising the other as a subject, we can only facilitate this through being in a third position. With the horse in the centre, it is easier for the therapist to take this third position, allowing the horse–client relationship to unfold as the subject–subject one. Benjamin talks of the task of the therapist to *surrender* to the third position, rather than obtain it – a position similar to Ogden's reverie and Bion's (1961) without memory, without desire stance.

In other words, in reclaiming our projections, we shouldn't try to push the horse out of the centre and relegate them to shallow beasts with prosaic capabilities. We must continue to allow the horse to occupy a space that keeps us open to their potential as a source of metaphor, bridging what is and what we observe to be. We need to stop fixating on Lady Shalott's mirror, accepting the curse of knowledge. But smashing the mirror entirely would be forbidding ourselves a rich source of perspective and insight. Allowing the horse to remain therapist helps us keep this third position intact.

De-centring the human

What happens when we remove the human subject from centre stage? One of the first things that people start talking about is whether horses pay attention to you or not. The fundamental issue with this is eye contact. Humans have eyes, in the predator's way, in the front of their heads, where horses have theirs on the sides of their heads. This means they have nearly 360-degree vision, but cannot see anything right in front or behind them. Because the horses are flight animals, one of the key steps to understanding is to imagine what it might like to *be* this horse.

An effective horseman needs to develop similarities to the horse; one of the most important of these is their vision. They must try to develop what Minette Rice-Edwards (2017) refers to as a "soft eye", as opposed to the hard stare of those who have their eyes central in their face as opposed to at the side. The soft eye is about taking in more of your peripheral vision. Once you start doing that, your eye becomes less focused on a particular thing at a time and you get in a different space with it all. You start becoming centaur.

The first level of observation is about what you are seeing and what is actually happening. It's an opportunity to get people to shift their attention from the huge things that they want to observe and see to the much smaller, subtle changes. This paves the way to communication, for they can have an opportunity to look at how horses relate to each other about what is it like to observe something you don't understand, that is quite subtle, and to bring in the idea of who is observing whom. Horses being flight animals, they watch very carefully whoever approaches them. At that point you get this realisation in the group that they are being watched as well. For the first time you bring the relationship aspect into it. That's why I always start with observation before relational, connections etc.; it brings a way of showing that this is not just me, there is also another. You need older children or adults for this exercise. The bigger the herd the better.

Observation then becomes a theme through the whole programme, whichever programme it is. It becomes about paying attention. All science starts with an observation; you notice something. What you do with it afterwards varies, but it always starts with an observation. So what people choose to focus on and what they bring to the observation tells a lot about the observer; they are not scientists in white lab coats trying to understand purely what the horses are doing, but they are actually disclosing to us quite a lot about themselves.

For example, people talk about the emotional relationships that the horses have: are they father and daughter? Are they brothers? Are they male or female? All of a sudden even for adults who know their biology, the sex of a horse becomes a confusing thing. The physical reaction to some of the horses' bodily functions can also be quite telling: the horse dropping their sheath, defecating, urinating, eating their excrement. Whether these things are commented on or not gives you a lot of information about the particular group: can they address it? Can they allow this "shit" to be part of their conversation? Can they tolerate it? Do they ignore it? In a sense, what they are observing is that there are going to be similarities in that horses have relationships and are clearly social animals, but also clear differences: the lack of reserve, disgust, or shame. This problematises the relationship between self and others – there is a level of disconnect that interferes with the clarity of the reflection we see when we look in the horse as a mirror.

There is often a level beyond the primary observation of those directly involved with the horses, in addition to the facilitator or therapists. These people are outside of the therapy or coaching group. They observe the behaviours of the individuals in the group, the horses, and the group behaviours generally and report those to the therapy team. Finally, there are the group participants themselves as they observe others carrying out the task and reflect on their own experience. One of the tasks we use to strengthen this as a separate, learning perspective is to split the group in two: one group's task is to observe in silence. This can give rise to competition and also to frustration if the task is protracted and rules are broken.

The position of the observer has a definitive effect on their understanding of a situation. For example, three horses are standing in a field, two together and one separate. To some the one on its own becomes the "lonely" or "sad" horse, yet for others he is the leader and the independent one. Equally, two horses standing together become the couple, the children, fearful, the bullies ganging up and pushing the other horse out. In truth, when we put ourselves in the system we cannot *know* what impact we have on the horses, we can only observe and experience.

Ryan came to us for therapy; he was sixteen, solidly-built, and wearing a high-visibility jacket because he was "dangerous". Within minutes, Philippa, a 28-year-old mare, went to him and put her head on his shoulder. This made me challenge my assumptions and accept in my mind an alternative discourse from the one that had been initially presented to me by the professionals charged with caring for him. In the narrative I hold, Philippa is a mother, an old mare; she clearly knows how to look after herself. She is not demonstrative yet with this unruly, over-sized child she demonstrates what I would perceive as affection. When I put this series of observations together, I allow myself to go beyond the high visibility jacket and feel affection for this child with the warning sign. This little vignette also encourages us to question the system that allows high visibility jackets to be issued in the first place. "High visibility" is ultimately another example of the result of a DSM-V classification, an elaborate taxonomy based on systematic observations as we point out in Chapter 1.

In sum, it is impossible to be objective when observing. There is always human agency, and I hope I have demonstrated that this subjectivity is something we must perceive in order to understand the helping power of the horse.

Beyond the word

An important shift to note is that we have side-stepped language in this process of observation. We listen, but perhaps we don't listen so much to what is being said as to what we *feel*. This is often a deeper kind of listening that doesn't hold language in the esteem in which it is usually held. We often confuse the origin of language. Language does not belong to nature; it belongs to culture. While we are born with the ability to speak, language is acquired as perhaps the most sophisticated human artefact. So if we push language to one side, what other types of communication can occur?

It is particularly useful to consider this when dealing with those who are diagnosed on the autistic spectrum. The label "autism" usually refers to a person whose development of a sense of self and a sense of others is altered dramatically. A number of explanations are available, including a dysfunctional emergence of the self, internalisation, identification, and introjection – yet no one theoretical account is conclusive. While US-originating approaches of behaviour modification are most prevalent in the UK, there is a growing body of interventions that reject deficit models and quasi-Pavlovian "rectification". Therapies involving animals in particular have made an appearance in this field.

Autism differs from other childhood psychiatric disorders in that there is a significant disconnection from the outside world. The disconnect is variously diagnosed as regressive or defensive, and mechanisms of social engagement that lead to identification are seen as crucial, including the dismantling of the ego, adhesive identification, and the bio-dimensionality of object relations. In particular, fear of a discontinuity between body and outside world is negated through the illusion of extrinsic merging.

Clearly, it is at this level that the horse as radical other might intervene. Young people can carry labels including the following, often with high co-morbidity: autistic spectrum disorders; pervasive developmental disorders; childhood autism (ICD-10); atypical autism (ICD-10); Asperger syndrome (ICD-10)/Asperger disorder (DSM-IV); non-verbal learning disorder (NVLD); right hemisphere learning disorder; semantic-pragmatic disorder; pathological demand avoidance (PDA); attention deficit/hyperactive disorder (ADHD); hyperkinetic disorder; attention deficit disorder (ADD); Tourette's syndrome; dyslexia; dyspraxia; developmental coordination disorder; motor coordination disorder; disorder of attention, motor coordination and perception (DAMP); fragile X; Rett's syndrome – this list is not exhaustive.

Science aims to be clear, yet much ambiguity remains, and it is here that we find the space to reframe the perspective and understanding of the individuals burdened with these weighty diagnoses. We operate beyond the diagnostic criteria and instead work experientially with any phenomeno-logical manifestation presented during the sessions. We don't centre the diagnosis, we centre the individual and their behaviours in the moment of interaction with the horse. For example, the notion that individuals may be able to speak but choose not to is a difficult one to grasp. It suits us a lot better to work with a deficit model – the idea that there's something missing, some lack – rather than a model that rejects and resists something we exer-cise agency over – people's right to choose how they behave, even if it's not socially "normal", and the equal merit of this alternative approach to life. See Higashida's account in *The Reason I Jump* below:

> When I was small, I didn't even know that I was a kid with special needs. How did I find out? By other people telling me that I was different from everyone else, and that this was a problem.
>
> (Higashida 2013, p. 15)

Higashida, an autistic boy who doesn't speak yet writes, gives an account of how for him his situation was only problematised because others didn't like it. He is quite bewildered why others would not respect his choice to silence. This is nevertheless a very controversial topic, in particular because of the popular perception of the refrigerator mother (Bettleheim 1967). This view, the dominant one until the 70s, held that autism was the result of ma-ternal coldness towards the child, thereby in effect stifling the emergency of a personality. While this view is now no longer seen as particularly useful, there is nevertheless an important kernel in the idea that is still useful – the notion that a choice, unconscious perhaps, is nevertheless possible.

Perhaps the most influential person in bringing Operation Centaur into being is Temple Grandin (1995; 2002). It was her background as a scientist, as well as being diagnosed as autistic, that allowed a profound revision of the condition, and brought together *interspeciality* as a potential intervention:

> I finally figured out that what Freud called the unconscious is the part of the mind that people with autism and animals think with. If one thinks without language one has to have sensory based thinking. I think in pictures; a dog may think in smells. Animals recognize other animals and people by voice. Even specific vehicles can be recognized. Sensory based thinking is true thinking. Budiansky (1998) provides an excellent review of animal thinking and cognition but he thinks that language is required for full consciousness. Research is making it very clear that animals think (Griffin, 2001). I hypothesize that in normal humans, language based thinking blocks access to more detailed sensory based thinking. Perhaps language blocks access to the unconscious.
>
> (Grandin 2002, *Evolution and Cognition*, p. 245)

As an articulate non-neurotypical researcher, Grandin has a great vantage point from which to make observations. Language, here firmly positioned as the cultural artefact it is, has no particular relevance to both animals and those who are non-neurotypical. Ultimately, not having access to language thwarts participation in social relations. Making it less valuable perhaps levels the playing field – this is the basic assumption of introducing horses into the intervention. To operationalise the above, we explore whether or how social communication takes place once language is side-lined. To this end, we ensured that no-one during the various sessions in the field or the arena spoke. For some this was easier than others. None of the young people, the horses and the therapy team spoke. The carers and volunteers needed constant reminding.

The case studies below come from one particular programme. For this programme we ran twenty-four sessions over eighteen months. Our team consisted of seven horses, one mental health professional, one equine specialist, two horsemen, one assistant groom, twelve teachers and carers and ten volunteers. The vignettes below give an illustration of what happens when language becomes de-centred, and the horse becomes the therapist.

Grace approached Jim, a twenty-something Shire horse, as she does everything in her life – her arm across her face, elbow pointing skywards, head bent to one side. She glances furtively at him. She is caught out that his eyes are on the side of his head, and briefly makes eye contact. Tears fill her eyes. In later sessions, she confidently stays on her own with two horses in the arena. She walks in the field with the herd and smiles. From the outside, not a lot is visible. Yet if we observe Grace close-up, we can spot a significant number of shifts.

Jack brings his football to the sessions, and the care team is about to take it away from him, as they believe it might scare the horses. I reassure them that is unlikely to happen, and in any case, we would deal with whatever happened. Jack is unusually animated with his ball amongst the horses. He is careful to wait for the horses to walk by before he kicks, and motions me to wait while horses walk past. Jack clearly has theory of mind. In other words, he can imagine what might be going on in our minds, suitably so in order to give us instructions. Teaching something to someone without the use of language is cognitively a very sophisticated activity. He kicks the ball to me, and he wants me to kick the ball back to him. As I pretend not to understand, he meticulously moves me in such a way that I learn how to play though his teaching.

Nicole is like a whirlwind when she enters. She tries to jump on the horses, but they won't stand still. Zoltan is with his mare, Philippa, and he sends Nicole away with a single head movement – she understands and backs off. In session seven, she tries to mount Jim, who stands at 18 hands. She climbs the fence to be higher. In session eleven, she again tries to jump on Zoltan. They enter a "dance", where both are turning so they keep facing each other. Zoltan gives several warnings, with head, ears and legs, which she appears to understand. Nicole climbs out of the arena and brings some grass, which she offers to Zoltan. He accepts the food, but when she then tries to mount him, he still prevents her from doing so. Again, this behaviour demonstrates a sophisticated understanding of social interactions. She wants to achieve something (getting on the horse's back), and tries a number of physical strategies before turning to psychological attempts – bribery by offering food.

Ahmed runs towards the big horse and beats him with both fists, hard. As he feels that the horse is not moving, a smile beams across his face. He gently kisses the horse. Ahmed comes to us labelled violent. He tends to lash out, throw chairs. The effect of the horse not moving, of being contained, created a very positive and gentle reaction in Ahmed. What is it like not knowing, or not being sure, where you start and where you stop? Feeling that you're reaching out to be limited, only to find everything moves away from you? Touching skin that remained standing still giving him the ability to connect grounded Ahmed.

Susie is nine years old. Born into a house that was used by drug users, to a mother who was using, she was locked in her room for the first four years of her life, without much human contact. While she doesn't speak, there is a real sense that an articulate person resides in her. She understands most things, and actions them almost immediately. As soon as she entered the stables, she was enamoured of the horses. One particular exercise, leading a horse for a walk in the park, is one of her favourites. She is joined by a group of her house mates, and as we walk with one or more horses, it is noticeable that the group becomes calmer, and becomes in sync.

When language is side stepped, the sophistication of the inter-species social communication comes to the fore. All participants with an ASD diagnosis were more responsive to horse cues than those who cared for them (for example, they picked up on ear movement, a key marker of a horse's intention). When social constraints are removed from them, these youngsters can explore what it is like to "be them" as they explore the horses around them. As observers, we move into their shell and observe their world rather than inviting them to join ours.

De-centring language is not only useful for those who can't or choose not to speak – it's just as useful for those who arguably speak too much. In order to learn how to deal with difference (for example, in our anti-bullying work, but also in corporate work when integrating new or difficult team members into the team), we remove language as a resource.

Silent Language of Leaders is a programme designed for corporate clients who want to develop insight into the way their teams operate. Originally piloted in Bangkok, I have now delivered this programme to many organisations internationally, large and small.

A particularly challenging task is when we ask participants to move the horses through a course or an obstacle without using language, neither with each other nor with the horses. All of a sudden, we have to try to communicate with an animal who doesn't speak our language, and whose language we don't speak, without using language. In some ways, people should find this easier yet most crumble. One particular exercise with a corporate group when this was the instruction, the whole group returned within five minutes stating it "was simply impossible" to complete this task. We had a useful conversation about giving up. It transpired that this group typically moved from task to task rather than attempt to understand difficulties. A different group realised that the horses represented a new member of staff whom they also struggled to connect with and to understand. When we have to connect with something new without knowing the rules, many challenges are presented – and many learning opportunities. Doing rather than talking in the first instance is a fundamental aspect of equine-assisted psychotherapy and coaching.

Conclusions

To conclude, I have shown that by de-centring the human subject and placing the horse at the centre of our observations, we get a clearer view of the other. Through understanding this other, who is now clearer in our vision, we are offered glimpses into ourselves. If we then further de-centre the human subject by eliminating language, we are observing a unique perspective where connection and relation can be explored in nature as opposed to in culture. Add to that the de-centring of the therapist, and we have placed the horse in the centre in three ways: beyond the focus on the human subject, beyond the speaking subject, beyond the subject of the therapist. This allows a radically different space in which to observe connections, roles and relations. Now we are de-centred, many exciting opportunities for understanding arise.

Figure 5 Sir David Attenborough meets our Shires as part of the *Harness the Horses* conservation and rehabilitation programme in Richmond Park.

Chapter 5

Interconnectivity

As part of a drive to control elk numbers, Yellow Stone National Park decided to reintroduce wolves to the nature reserve. Having been hunted to extinction because they didn't fit the surrounding agrarian culture, these predators were now deemed useful again to address an overgrazing problem. The results of this reintroduction were astounding.

The wolves' predation on the elk population, until then unchallenged, produced a significant increase of new growth in various plants. Aspen and willow trees, previously grazed by the elks more or less at will, got suddenly a chance to grow. With the presence of the wolves, the elks stopped venturing into deeper and for them dangerous thickets where they could easily be surprised. They began to avoid areas of low visibility, which would increase the chances of wolf attacks. The elks began avoiding open regions such as valley bottoms, open meadows and gorges, where they would be at a disadvantage in case of an attack from a wolf pack. With new vegetation growing and expanding came subtle changes in the waterways running through the park. That had an impact on other species as well. Various bird species came back to Yellowstone with the increased number of trees. The beaver, previously extinct in the region, returned to the park. Their dams across the rivers attracted otters, muskrats, and reptiles. Probably due to the wolves keeping the coyote populations at bay, the red fox suddenly got a chance to survive because the number of rabbits and mice grew considerably. The raven, always the wolf follower, came back to the park as well, now able to feed on the leftovers of the wolves. The wolves changed the rivers, in as much as they readdressed the lost balance within the region, one we had created when we exterminated them. With a better balance between predator and prey, top meat eaters and top grazers, came the possibility for other species to thrive. With the increased vegetation growth, erosion decreased and the river banks stabilized.

If wolves can change rivers, what can horses do with us – and what can we achieve through connecting with horses? The Yellowstone example illustrates how everything in nature is connected. While the initial hypothesis was that wolves would solve the elk problem, so much more resulted from this.

On the whole, we seldom take our context sufficiently into account. The way we interconnect is a vital part of conducting therapy or coaching with horses. These days, I very rarely see people in consulting rooms. They come out and see me in the park, not always to work with the horses. Walking during therapy or coaching has numerous benefits. First, we walk side by side, the closest you get to approximating the couch. The couch doesn't necessitate eye contact and allows the patient a free flow of associations unfettered by the cues of the analyst. Walking allows for the same effect. Second, there is movement. Many people turn to therapy because they feel stuck. Third, the park is a truly interconnected space. We're under the Heathrow flight path, there is traffic – but there is also nature. It's very hard to deny that you're being part of a system.

Interconnection

We connect with different parts of ourselves; with others; with the primitive and with nature. For example, children usually find the bodily functions of the horse hilarious – horses know no shame when it comes to farting. Their laughter serves as a release, a reminder that a rule, a boundary has been traversed. A connection has been made. A horse is allowed to be a horse.

Zoltan, the chestnut gelding, was standing diagonally in the shelter, to the right hand side, so his body was completely in the shade. Two further chestnut geldings were standing outside the shelter, facing Zoltan. As we approached, he left the shelter and walked to the gate where we were entering. We walked into the field and he resumed his position in the shelter. Later, he walked directly towards Patrick in the field. Patrick raised his hand to touch the horse, but Zoltan moved his head forward, as if in a nod. Patrick withdrew his hand at this, which happened twice. A little while later, Zoltan approached Patrick and very gently touched him briefly with his nose on the forearm and walked back to the shelter. The other horses moved out of the way so Zoltan walked back to his original spot where he remained.

At one level, this doesn't seem particularly remarkable. Yet in the context of a therapeutic process that centred on connections, or the lack thereof, it was an extraordinary turning point. I had been working with Patrick for over two years, on and off. He found connecting with others difficult and painful. Patrick wrote about the incident in a diary he shared with me:

> The horse masterfully demonstrated how to connect with others with strength, warmth and compassion whilst maintaining his own healthy boundaries and personal safety. We didn't talk or theorise about it: the horse did it in real time, there in front of me. I couldn't miss it.

Patrick talks of how the horse managed the pace of the connection between the two of them, slowing it down if Patrick was going too fast and taking time out as he needed for himself. He was, says Patrick, always aware of his presence even when he was physically further away. Patrick experienced the horse showing him how to take charge of the situation with elegance and self-possession. He wasn't giving away all his power nor totally dominating the situation. Patrick states:

> He came back close to me (but not too close) when he wanted to connect more visibly, having first taken his time to assess the set up. He blew gently on and touched my lower left arm when he was ready to strengthen the connection. He touched me with a gentle power that still blows me away. This is the part I remember most vividly.

At first Patrick saw this behaviour as an alternative model of how to act. Later on, he realised that the horse had shown him, deep down, who he is. Doing and being – Zoltan was perhaps not telling him what to do, but he was reminding Patrick of who he was. This session pulled together all the elements of connecting we had covered throughout the time I worked with Patrick. Zoltan summarised everything Patrick needed to know about establishing a healthy connection. While it was deceptively simple on the surface, Patrick felt he had been able to make something external internal, with easier access and permanence.

This example illustrates that in order to be able to develop an awareness and consciousness of self, there needs to be the existence of an other, and an other in which we are able to perceive consciousness. We project or express ourselves onto that other, and through their reaction, and interplay with continued expression, we are able to become conscious of who we are. Hegel refers to this other as an eye, which looks upon us. This hints that in order for us to define ourselves, we need to experience an interconnection with an other. We, in essence, define ourselves by the other, and are also defined by the other. There is a difference between who we think we are, and who we actually are. Our ability to perceive ourselves in our entirety is limited, so there is a creation of an internal gap in our psyche. Who we are, versus who we think we are. This internal gap is sometimes referred to as a lack, or a sense of incompleteness. Zoltan's connection with Patrick helped Patrick to understand this lack.

The external and the internal

One of the main functions of psychotherapy is making the unconscious conscious. Through expression in words, emotions and memories stored deep within us reach the surface and become knowable because they now also exist outside of us. Once uttered, these linguistic representations of what resides within can no longer be unknown. At a very early age, we learn to be both in our internal world as well as in an external one. Through good-enough parenting, we in effect realise we exist both in our mind and in a social structure.

What is inside us and what is outside is therefore not always experienced in a straight forward way, and the previous discussions on the divided self and the self versus the other have shown that this is not as simple a concept as it sounds. Connecting things requires a sense of where one ends and the other begins, and Lacan (1956) uses the notion of a Mobius strip to illustrate the interconnectivity of what happens inside and what happens outside. Evans (1996) describes the strip as follows:

> The Mobius strip is a circular strip with only one continuous surface and only one edge. Whilst initially the image of a Mobius strip may appear elementary its paradoxical nature becomes apparent when one imagines an object travelling across the strip's surface. From the object's starting position it will travel through a circle twice before arriving back to its original position on the strip having travelled across its entire sur-face, inside and outside, without having to lift from the surface itself. While illustrating spatial paradox, the Mobius strip draws attention to the actually cohesive nature of binary oppositions whereby either term (inside/outside, love/hate, etc.) cannot exist without the opposite.
>
> (Evans 1996, p. 119)

Lacan uses the Mobius strip to position his psychoanalysis beyond binaries. In other words, he demonstrates how opposed terms are continuous as opposed to categorical, and can therefore co-exist without a boundary. Examples of this include inside/outside, or love/hate. They cannot be separated, one doesn't exist without the other.

The function of the Mobius strip is to show that what is spoken and therefore conscious is connected to that what hitherto remained unspoken and therefore unconscious. This in effect demonstrates how the conscious relates to the unconscious, and gives us an understanding of how metaphor functions in this respect. Metaphor allows us a generic glimpse into what might be uniquely occurring for an individual. For example, Tamara gets trodden on by a horse. This literal act becomes metaphorical – what is it to be trodden-on? Tamara becomes very emotional and starts talking about how she always feels trodden on. Her mother never respected her space and was overbearing. Her first husband would hit her and she felt she had no right to stop him, or to even question. Tamara said:

> I felt a bit like he was doing what he wanted. I felt a little over powered. A bit trodden on. Thinking about it now, it reminds me of my

relationships with people. Due to my lack of confidence other people might do stuff and I don't always stand up for myself. It gets to the stage where it goes on for a while and instead of saying something in the beginning I end up exploding in the end.

Metaphor connects the inside and the outside – it becomes the bridge by which the unconscious becomes conscious.

Being able to transfer immediate experience to past and future experiences, and make sense of it, is an important skill in rehabilitation. The insight of "being trodden on" really made her reflect on the role she plays in relationships. On another occasion, the same Shire was crowding Sabrina. She struggles with boundaries, and in the session has a huge Shire horse towering over her. She feels overwhelmed – "I feel like a mouse," Sabrina softly states. I ask her why mice have to be timid. Initially reluctant and hesitant, she pushes back – and the horse moves back.

Sally sees the horse approaching her, and she immediately exclaims "Oh look she loves me – it's as if I'm a princess when they do that." Moments later, she continues to murmur, "She loves me, she loves me so much." My vision of this interaction was rather different. The piebald mare approached Sally with her ears pinned right back, pulling a face that in no uncertain terms indicated to back away. She didn't respect Sally's boundaries at all and in effect pushed her out of the way, not once but at least four times. This is what Sally was calling love. She tells me how she does everything for her husband, avoids doing things for herself, yet he still ignores her. She tells me how her adult children come into the house and order drinks and sandwiches. With the horse, she says, it's different, she feels loved. I ask Sally about being a princess. A little later, I offer Sally my understanding of the session, and point out that perhaps the horse is also not respecting her boundaries yet she experiences this as love. Sally breaks out in floods of tears – "I'm more of a Cinderella really."

James was originally part of a group from a pupil referral unit. The other group members were no longer attending, so I decided to work with him on a more individual basis. I asked him to complete three different tasks, in part designed with his previous experiences in the group in mind. Task one was to meet the horses and then return, an exercise designed to connect to others. Task two was to tell the horses a secret, which is designed to connect with memories and emotions, and usually shame features prominently here. Task three is a request to end the session by saying goodbye, which is a connection to loss. Connecting with a horse for the first time is an encounter with something more primitive, less edited but fundamental in understanding ourselves in relation to others. We often refer to this as gut feelings, which are usually dismissed and replaced with more "rational" accounts. As James entered, the two horses were standing at opposite sides of the manège. This was the first session we conducted in this space. A manège is in effect a sandpit, and as such it has references of play, exploration, both cultural connotations. It is also a boundaried space, as physically there is a fence around it, there is a gate, and therefore there is inside and outside. The gate forms the legitimate way to enter and exit. It's also a container, it contains one or more horses, various objects and eventually people as the participants and therapy team come in. It also has authority in a number of different ways: who comes in, when they come in, how long they stay and what task will be conducted is all "decided" by the therapist. In sum, there's a physical boundary, a time boundary and a task boundary. A bound space, a job to do and someone in charge. This is no longer a neutral space. James engaged with the first two tasks, somewhat subdued but nevertheless participative. When I gave the instructions for the third task, he quickly came back. "How stupid," he shouted, "this is just so stupid." When I asked him why, he shouted: "Because it's like talking to a wall, they don't listen!" James is attributing the wall to the horses or the outside world, but actually it is his wall that he is creating. Something was being touched around loss and endings, and he was not going to continue with that connection.

Internal/external walls, Cinderella/princess, mouse/shire, trodden on/ standing up – the idea of the Mobius strip helps us understand the way things are connected, and makes movement along the continuum possible. It gives us an understanding of where and how we are positioned. It even allows us to question the very boundaries through which a sense of self has been constructed.

Silent language of leaders: case one

The horse has to be able to habit our internal as well as our external worlds. They are a horse, but they're also part of us. In psychotherapy and coaching, being able to discern what is "me" and what is "not-me" is very important for emotional health and well-being. In order to achieve this, a number of equine-assisted situations are established that function to allow individuals and groups to take their projections back, thus achieving some more clarity and understanding.

When organisations are learning to connect, horses function as a great methodology. The usual communication methodologies such as meetings, memos and workgroups may address the linguistic and rational part of ourselves, yet don't address at all what is under the surface. A tech giant had seen some changes on its leadership team, including the appointment of a new Chief Executive. As part of a wider culture change programme we brought the team to meet the horses. How do you move from one state to another? Standing to walking, walking to trotting for horses. How do you shift something that is immobile and make it mobile? How do you manage the feeling of being stuck? I ask the team to connect with the horses. Instead, they very quickly connect to their anxiety – the feeling of powerlessness they experience. My request to move horses rendered them immobile.

One way of addressing this debilitating state was scepticism. I was asking the impossible of them; I was deliberately trying to make them fail; nobody can do this task; horses are stupid anyway. I sent them back to the horses with the original request, to connect. After a few of these iterations, fear become discussable. The group started addressing their projections. I was no longer the cruel person out to make them fail, the horses no longer stupid.

As a result of this, various aspects became discussable. We managed to establish there wasn't a motivation to work together between various members of the board, and they weren't making many attempts at sorting things out. The way this related to the horses and the task was that they gave up, rather than address what each of them wanted, and what they could uniquely bring to the task. Once we pointed this out to them, for the first time they could start contemplating things like division of labour and setting up different task groups. For the first time, someone was allowed to take a leadership position. To exercise one's authority can be a dangerous thing. Whoever takes on a leadership position opens themselves up to be attacked, both for exercising authority but also for daring to be different in the group. From this point, the group started to get organised and make a plan.

We managed to get people to acknowledge their judgements and make their prejudices explicit. It was easier to deny that they were there, than to acknowledge and work with the differences. People like to believe "we are all the same". But clearly, when the group involves horses, we are not all the same. We can no longer deny that there are differences in the group. Once we acknowledge that difference (facilitators, gender differences, level of experience), all of a sudden the fear is palpable. When we are younger, and edit-less, it is much easier to pick and choose and to discern difficulties. In picking sports teams in the playground, kids are ruthless at wanting the best, more powerful and more skilful in the teams. But in the modern organisation this may not be tolerated in the daylight, but in the shadows and under the surface it still continues. Calling on a management team and illustrating that not acknowledging this was the reason for not completing the task was a shock. The sessions with the horses paved the way for some important reflections. Very different personalities who were judging each other in a very black and white fashion had become far more nuanced in the way they experienced their colleagues. Some of their defences had dropped to the extent that having a meaningful conversation was now actually possible. Horses in their radical alterity made the fear of difference discussable. Once this was acknowledged, impotence turned into success.

The Human Resources team who were managing the team later told me that the group had worked as a group for a first time. They connected with each other. This connectivity brought many fruits straight away, as difficult meetings about resource needed to be held. To remember the intervention, they sent a photographer to take pictures of the horses to hang in the boardroom. A permanent connection with horses, with nature, and with each other.

Silent language of leaders: case two

A professional services firm experienced a disconnect between senior and middle managers, and wanted to find out why and what could be done. While talk, in a form of interviews, written accounts of organisation policies and data such as performance and productivity can give useful insights into how organisations function, nothing is more powerful than spending some time observing organisations and the people who constitute them as a blank slate. As discussed in Chapter 3, we are very much trying to make the familiar strange and the strange familiar. Long before anybody ever meets a horse, the lessons you learn from the field and the stable are already applied in the "field" of the organisation. Some of these observations lead us to formulate some hypotheses which we will use to design our days with the horses. As a team, we then discuss how close or far removed our observations are with what it is that the organisation has identified as the presenting issues. That gap is the first thing that we explore.

The presenting issue was that the senior management felt that the middle management needed to step up, as they were considered not productive enough. We juxtaposed this with our observation, which was that they are not working cohesively. There was a real sense of the two layers not connecting, and we wanted to explore why this might be the case. The gap then was between the view of unproductiveness versus incohesion. These views have very divergent origins: one views the cause predominantly at the level of one group of employees; the other takes a more systemic stance. We proposed a series of sessions, where we work with senior management and middle management separately, and then bring them together for a joint session.

As the group of middle managers arrived, Donna announces she is very afraid. During the safety briefing, I make clear that everyone is part of this group and it is entirely their choice whether they go into the field or not. People should not ignore their fear, and listen to what their bodies are telling them, I state. Horses don't really notice fences in that way. To them, a person is registered whether in the field with them or on the other side of the fence. I made it clear that Donna needed to make that decision. As it happened, the group somewhat decided for her, as they all left her behind at the gate. For the next forty minutes, no member of the group as much as looked at Donna. I made sure a member of my team kept her in vision throughout this time.

How did we make sense of this? Donna brought a very powerful emotion to the group – fear, or an overwhelming anxiety to the extent that isolation was preferable. The group had no desire to acknowledge this fear, and preferred it kept well away from them. Because Donna was expressing fear, and carrying it for that group, they didn't have to carry that around with them. Donna was doing something on behalf of the group, expressing anxiety and fear (in this case of the horses). There was no attempt for the group to address this in a constructive way whatsoever. What they chose to do was to split it off and cut it out, and look at it disdainfully. There was no acknowledgement that they had abandoned someone and that they were not following the instruction of working as a whole group in the task.

It is interesting to observe how people and groups avoid or face fear. In almost every group there is someone who expresses fear of horses. It is very useful to observe how the group addresses this. Do they leave them be? Do they force them in? Do they listen to the fear? Do they attempt to work with it, or do they ignore it? Whatever they do in the field is a very clear indication of what they do in the organisation. So while Donna expressed fear of the horses, we were curious where that fear was coming from, what it stood for in organisational terms.

After some questioning, it emerged that a culture of fear existed within the organisation.Historically, there had been a lot of blame and finger-pointing in the organisation. More recently, an all-hands meeting where senior management had publicly expressed disappointment at the performance of middle management made an indelible impression. Fear prevented middle managers from stepping up.

So very quickly we established what explained the gap between our interpretation (cohesion) and senior management's interpretation (productivity): fear. The problem for middle management was not about how to step up but about daring to step up. How can you take a risk? How to make mistakes in a blame culture? How can you be a little fearful and not let that stop you working as a cohesive group? This became the central theme to work with this group over the next few sessions. On one occasion, one group's task was to come up with a solution to a problem involving moving two horses. The other group was asked to observe from a distance. The observers couldn't hear what the task group were discussing, so after a while they assumed the working group had become disengaged with the task as nothing was happening. Eventually, however, the working group went on to solving the problem and getting the horses to where they needed to be. What the observer group had described as disengagement and laziness, was actually the working group building relationships and spending time articulating the problem and its possible solutions. This allowed us to bring in and discuss the larger themes of disengagement in the organisation from a shared experience.

The subsequent discussion of the two groups allowed for a number of useful insights, not only pertaining to working with the horses in the here and now but how both parties tend to be perceived in the organisation (what is true; what isn't true? How can we hold multiple perspectives?). When we then talked to the groups separately, the observed group felt it was refreshing to hear an unedited view of themselves; whereas the observers experienced the reality of multiple perspectives perhaps for the same time: "Because we are in such a senior position, we tend to assume that the world as we see it is correct. It hadn't occurred to me that it may be anything else," said one.

During one of the sessions, we took the middle management team through four sessions with the horses so that they could learn a lot more about how to build relationships and complete the tasks. On the final day, the senior management team were re-introduced to the field where they encountered a middle management team who they recognise, yet it feels very different. The playing field is no longer even; the senior management team now need to rely on the middle management team and their newly found expertise in order to complete the task. In the field, the seniors "dare" to listen to their middles; they are willing to concede that they know stuff about what they are doing. If they can now translate that knowledge to the running of the organisation, this would be a very successful intervention. They're allowing their employees to take their own authority; usually they don't see that they are blocking this, as there is also a fear from the senior management team about the authority of the middle. The fear of the authority is not unidirectional, is bi-directional. It also works from the senior to the middle team. The group managed to get a handle of their fear which allowed them to have a list of actions that better reflected the presenting symptoms. They managed to let go their attachment to the systems that they have identified as presenting symptoms in the organisation. We managed to allow them to identify some of the underlying causes rather than symptoms. This allowed them to move away from the status quo to a position of action. That is the best that any intervention can hope to achieve. What those action points are, are now to a certain extent immaterial. What the intervention with the horses allowed them to do is to change their position, become more autonomous, each and every one of them and experience that each has a responsibility for the collective achievement. It's not about a more senior person being responsible for delivery, it's something we all share.

Following the sessions, we received a postcard from Donna, who told us that for her this had been one of the most life changing events she had taken part in. She felt she needed to make some important decisions about her own choices. She no longer felt so scared.

Centaur Recovery

In the *Centaur Recovery* programme, we work with people who are struggling to understand and address their addictions. Mostly, these are patients that come to us as part of a wider treatment programme, typically including hospital-based primary interventions. Always a group intervention, we help identify alternative ways to manage difficult emotions as part of the addiction treatment through connecting with the horses. There are many different levels of interconnectivity during the sessions. First, there is the connection with the natural horse; then there is the connection with the representation of the horse; followed by the interaction, the challenge and frustration of a different other who doesn't follow the same rules; and finally, a re-connection with old patterns in one's self, combined with new understandings.

Connection with the horses, with their sheer physicality, their weight, size and smell is undeniably a connection with something outside of your self. Initially, the observation period of watching the horses interact with each other, or just being in their company, evokes powerful reactions. It is easy to take horses for granted when you are surrounded by them all the time. As a therapist, I prepare myself for these sessions by looking at these horses not as familiar colleagues but as strange creatures – without memory, without desire, as Bion would put it. I tend to use the two older Shire horses in the herd, gentle giants who do have their moments, but I trust them implicitly. There is something very grounding about them.

Safety

The safety briefing takes place at each session, and happens outside of the work space, either in the stables or outside the field or manège. It is an opportunity to ground people firmly in themselves, and indeed, post equine-assisted psychotherapy, 78 per cent of participants reported an increased awareness that their actions have consequences. This is the aim of the safety briefing – don't expect anyone else to take responsibility for your actions, and not acting on something may result in getting hurt. The safety briefing gets people in touch with their bodies, with their gut feelings. If you don't feel safe, do something about it, is my message. Later on in the sessions, the behaviour–consequences corollary resurfaces often.

When the horses don't want to move while completing exercises, patients learn they are the ones that need to readjust their behaviour.

> When we came together for the last challenge and how although our first plan was not working we kept going back to it, doing the same thing – and then we tried a different way. Then finally it clicked, we learned to do it differently and completed the challenge.

Connections and re-connections

Following the safety briefing I ask the group to go and meet the horses, to introduce themselves, to say hello in whatever way they feel they want to do that. This is the first time participants have the change to be touching and talking to the horses. While the instruction is clear, there is nevertheless room for interpretation. How exactly do you introduce yourself to a horse? Having that initial 1-2-1 time with the horses is important, because how people attempt to make the strange familiar is an important insight into their inner world. For example, some people recall the touching the horse for the first time, the first time a horse nuzzled them, as the horse "wanting more affection", which heralds the start of the transference relationship, and therefore the possibility of projections being observed, understood, and taken back.

Stillness and memories

"My head is like a washing machine" is a description often used, and I've heard this in prisons, in clinics, in schools. It appears that spending time with a horse can create some stillness, a connection to a quiet space, and a feeling that one is not alone but part of something wider – and this is experienced as soothing. Contemporarily referred to as mindfulness, in post equine-assisted psychotherapy 72 per cent of participants reported an increased focus on the here and now, and a sense of calmness. A further level of connection, as in prison, is with the memories of horses. This is important, as for many it counters the good/bad split of childhood experience. No matter how difficult and how hard things are to remember there were positive experiences to hold on to, too. "It was great to be around horses again after so long," said one participant. "Loved the horses. I was brought up on a farm so memories were happy," said another. Continuing to observe triggers recognition for some about their own behaviours – horses acting as mirrors.

> When I first approached them, they were not interested and continued to eat. Nothing else mattered to them, they were simply not interested and focused on their food. When I realised that was me with my bottle of wine it really touched me and made me cry.

Many discuss the behaviours in terms of the powerlessness they have over alcohol, and how connecting with the horses helps their understanding of the treatment and the barriers. Many reflect on how the horses are physical representations of addictions.

Connecting with emotions

One of the core struggles for anyone, and especially those addressing addiction, is connecting with their own emotions. The use of substances in effect has acted as blocking this connection, and following primary detox intervention, the rawness of newly felt emotions is challenging. Post equine-assisted psychotherapy, 77 per cent of our participants reported an increased in the openness to their emotions. "When I met the horse for the first time on my own, I felt this huge wave of sadness washing over me," said one person. "I cried for the first time in years as I hugged that horse."

> Right at the end of the session, and copying what I'd seen Andreas doing, I put my head very near the head of one of the horses. It very

slowly moved its head towards mine – in a sort of "hello" – and trusting gesture. It was very special! I could tell he trusted me, and despite his size, I trusted him completely.

Following the sessions, nearly three-quarters or 73 per cent of participants reported an increase in their trust levels.

Trust is crucial, as it forms the basis of a proper working alliance. It signals there is a reaching out to an environment that is now not solely perceived as hostile, and against which one needs protection. It acknowledges the existence of a less persecuting context, a less persecuting other. One, even, who can be trusted to help. The reluctance for those struggling with addictions to ask for help is well documented. Faced with a herd of horses, radical others, with no knowledge of how horses operate, we ask the recovery groups to create movement. The group tends to rush in, without discussion or making a plan – even consulting amongst peers is a hard thing to do.

Challenges in connecting as a group

The connection with and as a group follows as a second task. Participants usually find it a different experience to approach the horses as a herd. Equally, the horses can, too, react in different ways. At times they approach the group, other times they walk away, giving rise to powerful reactions either way – they love us, they hate us. Walking with a herd of horses in silence is a powerful experience. It helps to bond the group. Being with others in a similar situation to yours, building a team to work through new experiences, and being outside. Even joining hands and moving towards horses are for some expressions of intimacy that they have not experienced for a long time.

Once the strange has been suitably made familiar, I ask the groups to consider some further activities. This is usually the time when the first frictions emerge. The tasks at some level are simple and straight forward. I ask for movement and direction of the horses to a particular place. A letter in the manège, a corridor that has been built, where they go to or how they get there is really rather immaterial. It is the encounter with the horses' subjectivity – their otherness and strangeness, their unknown qualities – which this exercise taps into.

Participants often struggle with the task, make the same mistakes time and again, usually until the treatment team asks for some time out to process. When asked, "Why didn't you ask us for help?" a deep silence typically ensues.

Asking for help

Post equine-assisted psychotherapy, 67 per cent of participants reported an increase in their understanding of the need to ask for help. The importance of teamwork and asking for help cannot be underestimated. Letting people in to help is an acknowledgement of the other, and the limitations of self. This connection can be risky, as it involves emotions. Trust and anger feature frequently here.

At this stage, a different awareness of resources start being brought to the fore. I point to the group as a resource. Some members may have prior knowledge of horses, why can that not be deployed? Who else may have some expert knowledge? What about the therapy team? What tools are available? Have you tried making a plan?

There is usually some reflection on not wanting to make things too easy. I point out that things usually are hard enough, and to make things a bit easier is not always a cop-out, it's not always a trick question. Resources such as knowledge and tools are there to be used. Participants have an opportunity to reflect that they need to use all resources to stay sober. They need to connect with others. They need to reflect carefully on the obstacles in front of them. They first take a big step back, then study the obstacle and what it represents in life carefully, then take a small step forward. It works when they act as a team, and once the group is cohesive, the horses are generally happy to oblige, too.

Sometimes some creative solutions emerge – the idea to bring the corridor to the horses, for example, usually presented itself as a challenge. Is authority being thwarted? Are we being subversive? The moment I am asked whether this is OK, and I answer no rules are being broken, a childlike energy descends on the group. They have worked something out, something clever, a solution. Trying different approaches can lead to hitting upon the right solution, so patients are encouraged to not repeat things they have already tried and didn't work. They learn how using power and force is not always the best way to get results. A crucial outcome is for people to experience that most times to get different results, they need to change and alter their way of thinking.

Processing

As a result of interacting with the horses and with each other, patients experience the importance of communications, of telling others their thoughts. They learn to understand that there are different ways of communicating, and learn to reserve judgement on people and situations. For some, this includes trying to be more persuasive without being a bully or aggressive – finding their own voice. Post equine-assisted psychotherapy, 65 per cent of participants reported an increase in their ability to communicate their needs, while 84 per cent of participants reported an increased level of openness to feedback.

Working through, processing what happened in the here and now and how that resonates, also heralds some drastic changes. Following the sessions,

78 per cent of participants reported an increased ability to work through new challenges. It's not talk based, as for addicts especially, talk is a way of not having to engage, it can act as a defence. For example, many times patients will pick up on one instruction I give ("introduce yourself") and spend a long time discussing the ambiguity. As one put it,

> I found the lack of instruction unsettling and I don't know why – I didn't enjoy it so much, feeling like a trick. We didn't find out the horses' names or relationships which I am sad about. I did ask about it at the beginning.

Authority was experienced as withholding, and rallied against, rather than getting on with task engagement. Fortunately, my co-therapists are there and they are always my go-to. Go back to the horses. Walk the walk rather than talk the talk, go and do it. It is learning in the experience that allows the connection to be made.

Achievement

A great sense of achievement is experienced when learning does take place.

Whether it is walking the horses through the obstacle course, running with horses and jumping over the jump together, or getting the horses to walk through the corridor at the first attempt – the achievement of the actual task is secondary to the sense of achievement that is experienced of doing something different, and getting different outcomes as a result. By this stage, participants have struggled with differences, have had to come out of their shell and connected with their peers, with the horses and with themselves. These are emotional risks that are not to be underestimated, without the usual defence of the substance to guard against the possible minefield of being in the presence of and interaction with these others. Learnings and reflections on these achievements lead to patients being more mindful about what they are thinking in the moment about themselves and others. Many learn to be more mindful and patient, and especially with the things they cannot control. Start with yourself, don't worry about changing the others.

For many in recovery, shame and low self-esteem are endemic. Ending on a positive, learning note is important to aid the building of confidence and trust in the recovery process. "This was a great experience – I've never worked with horses and it's a great confidence builder for me to know that I can succeed in difficult tasks", is a typical response. Even those people who are initially sceptical clearly reflect on the benefits: "Although I've said that I won't do anything different after this session, it did reconfirm a number of things I am going to action when I leave treatment." Connecting and recon-necting can be a powerful intervention.

Figure 6 Teenager contemplating a Shire in Hyde Park, part of the *Real Horse Power* programme.

Chapter 6

Relations and roles

We are observing the Shire horse herd, all eight of them, in a forty-acre field at the back of Hampton Court Palace. Jennifer is nervous. This is only her second session and she specifically expressed an interest in working with the Shire horses. Many people do. They tend to represent something powerful, over and above other horses: power, might, tradition, nobility, work, Britishness are just some of the descriptors often attributed to them.

We begin the session by observing from a distance. I ask Jennifer what she sees. This part of the session tends to be the most revealing as it allows for many projections to come to the fore. It is not uncommon for people to state that nothing is happening – "they're just horses". If however as a therapist you can hold this moment and not intervene, very soon the client moves away from the literal space. Jennifer picks up that two of the bays keep running towards two black horses. She asks me what this means. Of course, we can never know what this means. I may have some interpretation in mind based on my knowledge of horse behaviour but that is not really relevant here. What is important is that Jennifer starts noticing relationships between the horses. I ask her what she picks up from the horses. "Those brown ones are bullying those old black horses" was her interpretation.

Are they bullying them? Whether horses can or cannot bully is immaterial at this point (I address this issue later in this chapter). Important here is that Jennifer now also attributes various roles to the horses. In the first ten minutes of the session she identified relationships between different coloured horses, and horses of different ages. Note that Jennifer does not know the ages of the horses. She also places some horses in the role of bullies, and others take the role of victims of bullies. Later on, she focuses on a young grey "irritating" an older grey. This gives us a number of insights. Using the horses as a canvas, Jennifer starts painting a picture of how she sees the world. She talks of struggling to find her place in life, her difficult relationships with her father, a now-ended relationship she experienced as abusive. Jennifer's focus on selective behaviours in the herd, and her subsequent observations and interpretations of roles and relationships, become our way into Jennifer's inner world. Horses, rather than dreams, become the royal road to the unconscious.

(Dys)Functional relationships

For the past twenty-five years, the focus of my work has been on relationships in all their vicissitudes. Perhaps more specifically, I have sought to understand how relationships form and develop and have the potential for dysfunction in them. The bulk of my research addressed notions of bullying. Whether in the school playground, the factory floor, family drawing rooms or the hot-desking office, relationships offer both the opportunity to be supportive and destructive. When I started bringing horses into therapeutic work, is was a logical step to utilise them in anti-bullying interventions. My work on bullying and destruction in relationships (Liefooghe 2001; Liefooghe and Mackenzie Davey 2001; Liefooghe and Mackenzie Davey 2010) illustrates the importance of naming something. In workplaces, for example, the term bullying is not solely used because the behaviour of a particular person, but rather to denote infantilising attitudes within the organisation – the term is bullying because it reminds you of school, it is as if you are treated as a child. This is important, as it takes the emphasis away of a relational dyad (typically, the bully and the victim) to something more contextualised – a group, a whole system, a whole organisation.

From minor family squabbles to nations at war, conflict is a universal fact of life, and one of its most potent features is the bully. To raise awareness of bullying, subtlety had to fall by the wayside – simple messages were important, and it clearly worked. Awareness around bullying, both in schools and at work, has increased considerably over the past two decades. Awareness, yes. But understanding? National Ban Bullying Day is held annually in memory of Andrea Adams and Tim Field, two pioneers who devoted their lives to eradicating bullying. Not so often mentioned is Adams' co-author, Tavistock psychotherapist Neil Crawford, who also died a decade ago. Crawford brought the subtleties of psychoanalytic thinking to the bullying at work field. "I feel I was robbed … my confidence disappeared," states a victim of bullying I talked to recently. Stealing is at the core of bullying. Envy, Crawford argues, involves identifying with the goodness of others and stealing it. Bullies are insecure, and feed off others, sucking the life out of them. Targets feel they are being robbed, feeling bereft, death. Sheila White, who continues and reshapes psychoanalytic thinking in the field, gives us the notion of the dance of death to understand workplace bullying. She describes it as a perverse and pernicious form of projective identification, occurring around organisational vacuums and structural fractures. Individuals, seeking recognition, get trapped in "a dance of death". Adult bullies do not have secure feelings about who they are, and through envy and the quest for recognition, hook into others and won't let go. Her book gives in-depth insights into the core issues of workplace bullying from the perspectives of the individuals involved, their interpersonal relationships, the group dynamics and – crucially – their organisational contexts.

Bullying will only occur if the organisational context is suitable for bullying. "Just as plants only grow if the conditions of the soil, temperature, light levels etc. are favourable, so bullying will only occur if an organizational context fosters a bully's need to bully", argues White. So what are these unsuitable organisational contexts? White describes organisations that have vacuums where there is no support for individuals or groups. She also highlights structural fractures, where job descriptions are unclear and communication is poor or inconsistent; expectations of performance are unrealistic and there is an over-identification with targets/quotas. Often, management are unaware of how negative projections filter down the organisation, generating the potential for dysfunctional behaviour along the way. Bullying is costly: increasingly petty conflicts are being registered as formal complaints and, in no time, legalities take over and costs spiral out of control. Preventive actions and interventions need to be based on a sound knowledge of the deeper issues which foster bullying scenarios.

My research since 1998 has consistently shown that to stop bullying it's not personalities but the systems and policies that need to be tackled – many of these are designed to cut costs, not to preserve dignity nor foster respect. Within these systems, managers are put under pressure to increase staff performance, reduce overtime, and cut costs to meet their targets – how employees experience this process is not top of the organisational agenda. BBC employees, like many others elsewhere, feel their respect at work is eroded by being kept in the dark, being serially restructured, not being consulted in earnest, feeling that sauce for the "grafting" goose is definitely not sauce for the "talented" gander. Many solutions seem designed to tackle only bullying of the inter- and intra-personal kind.

Part of coping with bullying is challenging the organisational practices that in an ever increasing, unrelenting fashion erode the self-esteem and self-efficacy of an entire system. What can be done to stop this organisational bullying and change a culture of fear? Arguably, the answer would be to question all organisational policies that are in place, and evaluate these in terms of their appropriateness for a dignified working life, balancing values with costs.

Do horses bully? A careful observation of their behaviours in herd shows behaviours of dominance, precedence, exclusion and status. For example, a horse higher up in the hierarchy will eat first, and will push other horses away in order to get to food. A new horse introduced into the herd will initially get kept on the edges of the herd and will not be tolerated too close. New horses may also get bitten or kicked as they find their place in the herd. Aggression is therefore very much present in horse-to-horse behaviour. That doesn't necessarily equate to bullying however. People observing from a human-centric perspective may see many examples of bullying. Place the horse central, and what you see instead is a set of behavioural rules that are clearly followed, ultimately with the aim of keeping order and safety. Survival of the herd rather than the individual. Power as a burden, a responsibility and anxiety rather than an indulgent position. Like humans, horses are social animals with defined roles within their herds. They would rather be with their peers. They have distinct personalities, attitudes and moods; an approach that works with one horse won't necessarily work with another. At times, they seem stubborn and defiant. They like to have fun. In other words, horses provide vast opportunities for metaphorical learning, an effective technique when working with even the most challenging individuals or groups.

So-called "difficult" or "bullying/bullied" children need to be contextualised, too. Schools, as they become ever more pressured by the expectation of better and better results, are reducing learning to a quasi-automated process. Knowledge has become a product, and if you disrupt this process, you become excluded. Schools on the whole do no longer contain. Focus on achievement dominates and pushes away safe places to learn and experiment, failure is no longer seen as a learning opportunity, but as something that needs to be removed. This pressure is as keenly felt by teachers and leaders as it is by their students, of course.

Menzies (1960) seminal study on social defences showed us how easily humans are reduced to functions and pathologies. As schools face oblivion or triumph in league tables, pupils are no longer seen as subjects but as part objects – some contribute to a place in the sun, others don't. The latter are outliers on the spreadsheet, and need to be removed to ensure they do not adversely affect the school's overall performance. Form-filling and box ticking replaces learning, and becomes a degrading model by which to measure both students' and teachers' performance. In an age where we count everything, from calories to anxious thoughts, being different from the norm is simply not tolerated. Against this backdrop, we encounter those that don't fit. Those that disrupt, those that are more vulnerable, those that bully. I designed the *Real Horse Power* programme specifically to counter some of these general, organisationally-held ideas and assumptions. That competition does not preclude collaboration, envy can coexist with cooperation and praise, and aggression is just as valid an emotion to be understood as is compliance. As we saw in the previous chapter, exploring how things connect is vital for a healthy and examined life. Bringing our horses into these excluded groups sought, paradoxically, to bring some humanity back in their experience.

Real Horse Power

It's difficult to bully a horse, particularly if we consider some of our Shires weigh over a tonne. Which is why we select these horses to run *Real Horse Power*, our anti-bullying intervention. Bullying steals self-confidence and belief for all concerned, and should never be tolerated. Even though we'd like to, we cannot make bullying disappear – to eradicate bullying is a non-starter. What we aim to achieve is to manage bullying in relationships to such an extent that the more extreme behaviours are simply not tolerated, and not part of the group culture. Our approach with the horses therefore, was to equip a whole group with the necessary skills to contain and challenge bullying and negative behaviours – whether they might be taking up the role of bully, target or bystander.

Equine-assisted learning sessions demonstrate how social relationships work in a herd of horses. Horses are powerful animals, and bullying tactics simply don't work with them. Instead you have to learn about cooperation and negotiation. Working with the horses is a great way to experience difference. Observing a herd of horses teaches us about the different roles all of us play in a group. It also teaches us that our behaviours are not fixed and can change – and that patience and communication are important if you want to succeed.

Cooperation may seem more laborious and difficult to achieve, and doesn't give the same short-term relief as conflict – yet once achieved, the psychological rewards are palpable. Horses will not cooperate when the groups are not cohesive, and we used principles of cooperative group work (Berdondini 1999; Berdondini and Smith 1996; Berdondini and Liefooghe 2005) to devise our programme. When the herd and group meet, there are continual learning opportunities regarding fear, trust, cooperation and competition. Each student will have to fund their space in the mixed human/equine herd. By working through a series of tasks, challenges and obstacles, they will observe a range of behaviours in the here and now and process them appropriately to arrive at non-confrontational solutions.

The sessions

Equine-assisted learning provides a space to explore ourselves in relation to others. Through noting the shifts of the horses' behaviours, their patterns specific to the group, their unique behaviour and discrepancies in the context as well as our own emotional and cognitive reactions to what happens, we build a series of hypotheses that we offer to the group for exploration. This learning is powerful and immediate. Participants are very often curious as to how the horses are related. This gives rise to numerous useful projections and fantasies about the horses. Are they brothers? Is there a mother and child relationship? Do they hate or love each other? Each speculation about the nature of the horses' relationships with each other becomes a useful avenue for the therapist or coach to explore.

The overall themes and objectives of our anti-bullying programme are to encourage the participants to take responsibility, manage new or difficult situations positively, challenge prejudice and discrimination assertively and develop emotional intelligence. Taking responsibility and being accountable is about recognising that actions have consequences. Horses give immediate feedback, which allows for participants' heightened awareness of their own behaviours, thus encouraging them to take increasing responsibility for themselves, their choices and behaviours. In particular, we focus in the sessions on how to make positive contributions to the group and participate in decision-making. We also spend time introducing participants to new and difficult situations positively, and model how these can be managed. That way, we offer experiential opportunities for participants to recognise, develop and communicate their qualities and skills, and understand and develop the range of skills needed for teamwork. We also challenge prejudice and discrimination assertively, by using the horses to explore and value differences between horses and people, thereby developing empathy. We move from a right/wrong way of split to a more integrated and complex frame of mind, one that can deal with challenges and accommodate difference, and that allows the discussion and analysis of social and moral dilemmas. Finally, the horses provide an opportunity to connect emotionally, thereby offering the opportunity to develop emotionally by identifying, articulating and managing feelings. In turn, this leads to the ability to form and maintain effective relationships that can be negotiated and re-negotiated. Following the Operation Centaur model, we look at how we connect, reconnect, move and direct.

Connections

Connections in many ways are about making the strange familiar. The object of the first session was to establish a baseline for the work. This involved creating a safe space in which to work. Our philosophy discouraged anything negative ("don't do this") and was cooperative and inclusive instead. It respected choices, brought people in yet also pointed out that all behaviours and all decisions have consequences. The way individuals and groups take the first steps towards building a relationship tells us a lot about both their internal and external worlds. Are you careful? Do you go in all guns blazing? There was a marked difference between groups – some stormed in and went straight for the horses, others initially didn't want to come in and stayed behind the gate. Of course, there were many individual differences too. Some displayed a lot of bravado on the other side of the fence, but once inside retracted their plans of "riding the horses" quickly. An encounter with a one-tonne plus Shire horse can be daunting indeed.

The time it took to familiarise themselves with the horses differed markedly as well. In one particular high-energy group, someone even tried to climb on top of a horse within the first ten minutes! In a different group, most walked towards the horses but didn't touch. We pondered how close you need to be to make a connection? Do you have to touch? Do these connections still endure when you are far away? This gave an important opportunity to learn more about the different attachment styles in the group, which in turn gave us an indication of the level of anxiety experienced in the group. Anxiety of course relates closely to being and feeling safe, hence safety was from the start an important topic. How can you keep yourself safe with others you don't know? In particular if they are really big, and you know they may kick or bite? Negotiating whether we are safe is an important skill to learn, and was a recurring motif in the programme. Every time a new horse entered the arena we drew attention to this. After a while, there was a consensus that only one's self can really ensure we are safe, and we should listen to our gut feelings about this.

Re-connections

Re-connections were made using the same two Shire horses as in session one. This session is to observe how horses function in the here and now, and to understand that they do not necessarily behave the same week by week. A large focus of the session is on managing difference, and how this can potentially create conflict and discord in groups. For example, when in one session three new horses were introduced, we had a revolt on our hands. Some participants refused to enter, and some called us "cruel" not to have brought "the old horses", forcing them to "start from scratch again, it's not fair". Participants found it difficult to factor in that, although their relationships with the Shire horses were beginning to build, there would need to be an ongoing investment and adjustment to the new relationship with the new horses. Many in the various groups find investing in relationships hard and are not always willing to stick at it. This frustration showed when for example horses were referred to as "not listening". A teacher recalled that her group were absolutely knackered after the session, emotionally and physically and all agreed that relationships are harder than they thought. In sum, the simple act of introducing and reintroducing different horses into a group allowed for some significant work to be undertaken regarding the nature of relationships, how self and other relate, and how we can manage to tolerate our frustrations even when things get tough.

Movement

This third session included movement. It also involved an appreciation of the new, as two grey horses were introduced, Henri and Homer, both 16 hands. The task is about mobilising a group of horses and people and leading them through a particular path. We split the group into two, and each group has to lead horses through a concourse, using all resources available, including jump stands and poles. We gave no further instructions as to how they have to do this – the groups have to decide for themselves. This session is relevant for young people to understand how we sometimes take clear communications for granted. Horses don't speak our language, so we have to communicate clearly to them in other ways. We were interested to see how the children would handle failure when they could not complete the task – and what they would do to prevent this.

Getting horses to move is a metaphor for creating change. How do you move a Shire horse that weighs more than a tonne? Cooperation rather than force will no doubt be required. Initially, this task is typically rejected as impossible. It takes a while before the various groups can find their own agency, and start experimenting. Some groups clap their hands, some groups stand in front of the horses enticing them, while others attempt to lead them by walking in front, showing the way. It doesn't take long before someone pulls a branch of a tree and attempts to feed the horses. We remind them of the no-feeding rule. This triggers a useful conversation on seduction and bribery – if a relationship depends on you giving a reward all the time, what do you do if you don't have rewards? Is that a solid relationship? "Not feeding" provokes strong reactions, and comments tend to range from "you're cruel" to "poor horses". There are a number of reasons we do this. Our horses have to work with a wide range of people, including young children. We don't want them to associate a human hand with food, and therefore start biting when none is forthcoming. More fundamentally, and more counter-intuitively, is the observation that giving horses titbits creates discontent in the long run. Horses that are used to getting apples and polo mints typically start making demands for them as soon as they notice a human. This results in stable yards full of door kicking. The fleeting satisfaction for the human and the horse of having a morsel of food results in hours of discontent waiting for the next morsel to show up. It can be very disruptive, too. The presence of an (unauthorised) apple in the manège created a fight between otherwise harmonious horses. We even had an example of a man trying to bribe a horse by offering a horse grass while it stood in a field full of grass. Clearly, food and feeding is never just about the substance, but about the role it plays for the individual and their relationships.

However, the tree branch referred to above also leads to a discussion of resources. What other resources are available? While there is some variability in time, all groups eventually discover the horses' head collars that were hanging from the gate. Having tools is one thing, but knowing how to use them quite another. This was the time when some useful conflicts started manifesting themselves.

Direction

The fourth session focused on direction. How to lead and how to follow? This session again used the two greys, Henri and Homer. Part of the challenge is to learn how to motivate a team and how to lead. The exercise, directing horses to specific points in the manège, allows budding leaders to find out if others follow. It also tests resourcefulness and questions what to do if the first plan doesn't work. This is a challenging exercise and really exposes people's character and skills. Navigating a group of horses isn't easy. Will the students use all the physical resources that were available e.g. the head collars hanging on the gate of the manège? During the final session, we once again built on previous weeks – but this time, the students could not use artificial aids or talk. The movement and direction of the horses had to result solely from the students' cooperation, energy and resourcefulness. While patience at times is tested during this exercise, focus is firmly on group work prevailing and task completion.

One of our major tasks was to ensure the group kept focused on the task at hand. And, of course, the horses were a great help with this. In effect, keeping a horse's attention is not unlike keeping the attention of someone with behavioural challenges. It is important to keep their attention on the task, otherwise they won't cooperate. A number of participants started making the link between the horses and their classmates: "that horse is just like you, he's bored quickly" and "neither of you (horse and human) are listening to what I say". So the exercise "move the horses" facilitated a big shift in the group – they were able to start thinking metaphorically. The horses may just represent me, and my feelings towards and thoughts about them may also reflect something about me.

What is the point of being able to create movement in others, if they cannot be directed? This session addressed the frustration the groups experienced the previous week by highlighting the importance of planning before acting. We constructed a "corridor" in the centre of the manège that would function as the place where plans were made, negotiated and discussed. We reached the point where we now had to take the other's perspective and become more in tune with them. Therefore, we were now no longer touching the horses or using language to communicate. For many, this may seem like a simple process. Not so – many senior executives don't get this right! For these kids to achieve this at the end of five weeks was an amazing achievement. Each group got there in the end.

The groups reflected on how the skills learnt on the programme could be transferred to benefit them in different settings and scenarios. Different roles were discussed, and surprise was expressed that people behaved in a very different way in school than they did in the manège. There were reflections on the conflicts that were experienced, particularly when different ideas, approaches and strategies were discussed and negotiated. Leadership and followership were crucial aspects to learn. Finally, planning and the resulting cooperation.

Being different and fitting in

It is not only bullying and conflict relationships that are encountered. Many of the participants in *Real Horse Power* are members of Pupil Referral Units. Organisationally, these units hold the pupils/students who need more specific attention for their learning. In practice, it is young people who disrupt the learning of others who find themselves here: students who are different.

Difference can manifest itself in many different ways. In one case, half of the group had worked with horses before; the other half had never seen one – were they going to help each other? Those who were new to horses were initially hesitant and anxious, which expressed itself in nonchalance, a refusal to leave bags and mobile phones and therefore a refusal to enter the sand school. Once we told them they did not have to enter, that they were still part of the group on that side of the fence, they started one by one to leave their possessions and enter through the gate. This was the first big achievement. Their difference could be acknowledged, and they could fit in unproblematically.

Magda stood out as different when everyone walked towards us, the only black girl in the group. She was also very confident, establishing a connection with the equine therapy team very quickly. She offered to assist straight away, and was very keen to engage with the horses. Magda was fascinated by the horses, and observed them in a very detailed way.

Instructed to form a herd of horses and people, participants quickly encountered what we call "the other" – something outside of ourselves that is both radically different but also strangely familiar. Magda experienced a lot of frustration about being singled out by the group as different. One example of this was that everyone else in the group spoke a second language she didn't know, so she was excluded from conversations. I brought this point home to the group by speaking a language that no one knew. This allowed a conversation about difference and about communication. We brought it back to the horses, as they communicate but don't speak English, nor French or Arabic. We collectively decided to communicate in silence from then on. Working alongside animals raises a range of important issues of how they are viewed and about being different. Do we see them as equal to us? Are they subordinate to humans? Do they have a place? Are they seen as subjects with feelings and individuality, or as functional and homogenous objects?

Fitting in is not surprisingly a key theme that emerges when working with these groups. Magda hadn't quite found her place yet at school yet. One of her teachers mentioned: "One of the first things I noticed was how Magda managed to fit in the group, because at school she's obviously finding it very difficult to have friends." Magda began to be accepted by the group when she demonstrated her leadership. Another teacher observed:

> A perfect example was when Magda suggested a plan to bring the horses to the path. She led the group and told us what to do and where to go, and it was a success. Everyone could see the joy on her face. She experienced fitting in for the first time.

Often, participants show a particular behaviour in the programme but do not transfer the learning into real life. We asked Magda's teachers to reflect on her behaviour a month after the programme ended. At first, the teachers focused on her accomplishments:

> With the horses she had a real sense of achievement, she could work with others, she could make friends, people listened to her. The sessions made a big difference for her. At school, she could reflect more and contain her emotions. She doesn't have the big outbursts she used to have before the programme. It's all a lot more measured.

Another teacher commented:

> Magda found her place. Before the programme, it was difficult for her to make friends. Now, she is just happier with people around her and she has definitely taken things away. Our relationship is now really different, we have a common experience that makes life at school a lot easier for her.

Connecting emotionally

We have evidenced that through building relationships with very different "others" such as horses, students began to take responsibility for the role they play in the group. The importance of this kind of reflection cannot be underestimated. The group had to learn how to plan and work cooperatively in order to achieve the tasks, when exposed to new and challenging situations. How to complete these tasks brought to the fore differences in opinion and, as a consequence, conflict. Participants had the opportunity to experiment – to try out new roles, to find trust. The latter is perhaps the ultimate aim of the human subject's desire to seek to connect and relate with another subject – to achieve trust in relationships.

Sometimes it helps to have a physical boundary. With horses, whether an electric fence in a field or a wooden post and rail fence around the sand school, there usually is a physical demarcation of space. Within the space, certain rules apply – staying within the space; not hand feeding the horses; regard for one's own and others' safety. It is also a space with a task. Of course, denoting the space, the rules and the task within it implies a further important element – authority. Ahmed's energy upon arrival clearly marked him out as a leader in the group. While small and one of the younger members, he presented a strong independence. It became clear that he had little regard for authority in any shape or form. We knew from this point that getting Ahmed on board would be pivotal to the success of the intervention.

From the very beginning, Ahmed challenged all boundaries and tasks provided. There were a small number of rules in the programme, but he challenged them all. For example, the gate needed to remain shut, so he tried to persuade the gatekeeper to open it for him; horses couldn't be hand fed, so he offered branches from the trees; and certain tasks needed to be done in silence, so he spoke loudly. Ahmed actively sought out those with authority with the aim to challenge. He particularly sought me out, as I was leading the sessions, to contradict, ignore and disrupt. Ahmed clearly had a lot of skills and enthusiasm but his distrust of authority seriously impeded on his ability to function – and in particular, to take up a position of authority himself.

At certain times, participants followed Ahmed's lead. As the group nearly completed one of the tasks, Ahmed yelled at the top of his voice which resulted in the horses veering off. The group became annoyed with him and called it a "malicious prank" – an act to disrupt or "sabotage" what the group was trying to achieve together. Ahmed became very withdrawn and refused to talk for the rest of the session. He vowed never to come back. We discussed the idea of disruption and sabotage with the students. The group reflected on how they now all had to cope with the "defeat" of not being able to complete the task. According to his teachers, Ahmed later declared "I do not like people who do not know me to tell me off, as they do not know me like that to do so". He was referring to a question I asked him at the end of the session – "Why did you yell during that session?" Clearly, he interpreted this not as an attempt to understand him, but to discipline him.

To gain authority, and indeed to experience one's own authority and autonomy, we first need to acknowledge that there is an authority outside of us. It was this acceptance that was the biggest and most central struggle for Ahmed. The pivotal moment came when he recognised that I was exercising my authority with the horses – they were listening to me, working with me, doing whatever I asked them to do. All this was achieved without touching and talking, no shouting, just silence. Ahmed became fascinated by how I was guiding the horses in a very subtle way, and how they cooperated fully with me. He realised that, if he wanted to lead, he needed to learn from me. To do that would require him to accept my leadership.

The results of this change were astounding. Ahmed started listening to me, and began asking me questions in a soft voice. Ahmed observed carefully in silence and understood how I was moving and directing the horses. At that point, he called the group back to the corridor (the only place where conversation and discussion can take place) and briefed them on his plan. The group went out under Ahmed's leadership and completed the task in five minutes.

To unite a disparate group is a great achievement. Ahmed succeeded because he was courageous enough to acknowledge his role in the large group, as someone needing to learn and to follow, as opposed to someone who disrupts others and sabotages what the group is trying to achieve.

Through this, he freed himself from the constant need to battle with authority and became "his own man", someone whom others trusted to lead them.

In the post intervention reflections, we asked Ahmed's teachers if the sessions had impacted on him, as it was clear to us that his attitude had changed. Ahmed was amazing in the discussion; he said that at the beginning he thought the task would be challenging, and he recognised "it was not easy", but felt proud they were able to accomplish it. He acknowledged it was the first time he felt the group worked together as a whole and "it felt good". Ahmed talked about the group working as a team, having a plan, looking and listening to each other. He was proud of his achievement.

Struggling with authority takes an extraordinary amount of energy and creates anguish and anxiety. This is often expressed as anger, with maximum disruption as the main intention – if I can't be in charge, no one else will either. Horses, as powerful beings who only accept being led in a cooperative relationship, are excellent teachers in understanding the dynamics around authority: to accept the rules of the other and, at the same time, enjoy your own autonomy.

Evaluation

Ahmed tried following rather than attacking authority, and recognised that his actions had consequences. Magda's case demonstrated that being different doesn't mean to give up your identity and become the same as everyone else. On the contrary, by recognising, developing and communicating her qualities and skills, she managed to fit in with the group without having to become like them. Overall, teachers commented that the groups were more able to identify, communicate and manage their own feelings and emotions, as well as others. It is this kind of emotional intelligence that we aimed to nurture. Cooperative groups can explore and value differences between people thereby developing empathy. We have shown that participants developed a range of skills needed for teamwork, and struggled with leadership challenges, as they came to understand both themselves, each other, and the horses.

A key aim of any psychotherapeutic intervention is to allow individuals to connect with and manage their emotions. During the debrief we asked all the young people to reflect upon their experiences during the sessions. Noticeably, a lot of attention was given to internal states and the core themes that emerged were trust, fear and confidence. "When you trust the horses, they feel it and trust you back," said Jackie, while James learned that "Trust is communicated without touch or words, they just feel what you feel." Zahara mentioned that "Only when there is trust between you and the horses you can make things work," and Philip likened the horses to his teachers: "When you trust them and they trust you, you become able to do things that otherwise you couldn't do." Many expressed a surprise that fear was such a big part of the initial sessions. Used to seeing people full of bravado, Emily felt "surprised to see people who generally seem very confident at school being so terrified in the horse sessions." Horses are great at bringing out latent emotions. In bullying situations, it is often fear and anxiety that lies at the root of the behaviours. "I was terrified, but through the sessions my confidence grew," stated Billy.

I was particularly pleased to hear the feedback on doing things differently. One of the core assumptions of *Real Horse Power* is that doing things collaboratively makes working together so much easier – it's hard to be in conflict all the time. In each group we worked with, the realisation that "only when we collaborated as a group the exercise worked" was the pivotal learning outcome. Participants had discovered they can change, they can do things differently, and it is more enjoyable. Tabitha observed "We are very loud in class: silence allows even more shy and quiet people to have a space and do things." This was echoed by Sylvia: "Horses need silence and quietness and this left space to be able to interact with each other."

An awareness of this range of emotions is relatively rare in this age group, particularly when raised in a group. These comments do explain the higher levels of pro-social behaviour reported following the interventions, and a reduction of more overtly aggressive behaviours.

Teachers' accounts formed a crucial part of the evaluation. One teacher stated the project had been a positive experience for three groups of pupils taking part:

> The activities with the horses have broken down some huge barriers for some of our students. They have had to think about and change their approaches to some tasks, understanding that their behaviour is a big influence on how the horses interact with them. It has been lovely to see some members of the group, who were initially very tentative about being near the horses – let alone touching them, being comfortable enough to work with them in an unfamiliar environment.

While another mentioned:

> It was lovely to see those students who were initially tentative about being in the arena, develop their self-confidence as the sessions went on. For some of the older boys, they had to change some of their behaviour so that the horses would work with them. This was a big step for them as, in the arena; the loudest person was not in charge. For me, this was the best part of the visit.

In addition to qualitative evaluations, we also measured pre and post intervention using two scales from Rigby and Slee's (1993) Peer Relations Questionnaire. These measured attitudes towards and behaviours towards others.

While the measurement before the intervention shows that teasing, spreading rumours, telling lies, picking fights and encouraging others to fight and spread lies were tolerated, these were markedly less tolerated following the interventions. There was also more acceptance of pro-social behaviours following the intervention. Overall, following our intervention there was a 62 per cent shift in attitude in line with our expectations that bullying would come to be regarded as unacceptable. Furthermore, it involved virtually the whole group, with 83 per cent of the group accounting for this change. A further scale measures the frequency and intensity of bullying-type behaviours pre and post intervention. Items in this scale include "I give soft kids a hard time", "I am part of a group teasing others" and "I enjoy upsetting wimps" – all of these items were reduced following the intervention. However, those that were reduced most pronouncedly were "I like to show others who's the boss" and "I like to make others scared of me". This indicates that there was a trend towards accepting our hypothesis that the intervention effectively reduced bullying behaviours.

Items in this scale include helping others, sharing things, making friends, and standing up for those who are being harassed. The scores on this scale increased considerably following the intervention. This indicates that there was a trend towards accepting our hypothesis that the intervention effectively increased pro-social behaviour. This is substantiated by the teachers' comments in the qualitative part of the report. The measures indicate that attitudes towards the morality of tolerating bullying changed drastically. An overall shift of 62 per cent showed that the students no longer tolerated behaviours such as teasing and fighting. Importantly, 83 per cent of the sample accounted for this shift, indicating that the vast majority had changed and that the change was not simply due to a few individuals. Their attitudes towards reporting wrong doing also changed, with most increasingly believing post intervention that reporting negative acts was the right thing to do.

Real Horse Power at its best.

Figure 7 Shires mowing the wildflower meadow as part of *The Centaur Club*, Kensington Palace.

Chapter 7

Work

A working connection is a particular kind of connection. Erik Erikson (1974) tells the story of when Freud was asked what constituted a happy, healthy life he responded, *to live and to work* (lieben und arbeiten). Whether these are actually Freud's words are debateable, but nevertheless, they point to the fact that these are two cornerstones of a contented life. In general, it is the love aspect that gets most attention, and this chapter seeks to redress this somewhat. Work, whether paid or unpaid, is good for our health and well-being. It contributes to our happiness, helps us to build confidence and self-esteem, and rewards us financially. A review by Waddell and Burton (2006) confirms that our physical and mental health is generally improved through work. We tend to recover from sickness faster and we are at less risk of long-term illness and incapacity when in employment. Conversely, being out of work has been demonstrated to have a negative impact on our health and well-being. People who are unemployed typically have higher rates of physical and mental health problems. Many take more medication and use more medical services, and have a shorter life expectancy.

Functions of work

Why is this the case? Waddell and Burton (2006) suggest there is compelling evidence that bringing people back into work leads to improved self-esteem, improved general and mental health, and reduced psychological distress.

Firstly, work gives us a purpose. It keeps us busy, challenges us and gives us the means to develop ourselves. Work also gives us a clearer identity, a sense of personal achievement that can lead us to be proud of what we do. Secondly, work can act as a strong motivator. There is a reason for us to get out of bed. Knowing that we have certain challenges to face can act as a strong motivation, and can counter a range of mental health conditions such as anxiety and depression. Not in the least because, usually, it also provides us with financial independence to support ourselves. Thirdly, work is a source of relationships – work enables us to socialise, build contacts and find support. Finally, work has rules and regulations, and why this may be difficult and a source of disagreeableness for some, it nevertheless provides a boundaried and safe space.

Of course, various physical and psychosocial aspects of work can also be hazards and pose a risk to health. Nevertheless, people in work tend to enjoy happier and healthier lives than those who are not in work. Work meets important psychosocial needs in societies where employment is the norm. To therefore not be in work makes an individual particularly vulnerable. This is why we developed *Harness the Horses*.

Horses are large, imposing animals that can weigh anywhere from several hundred kilogrammes to a ton. They are also social animals, just like humans, and they have defined roles within their herds. Horses have distinct personalities, moods and attitudes. What works with one horse will not necessarily work with another. A horse may seem stubborn and defiant, or playful and fun. Horses require work. In a domestic setting they can't clean or groom themselves, or set out their own food. And attending to their needs requires discipline and responsibility.

Harness the Horses

Harness the Horses is a programme is for people in transition, either unemployed, homeless or both. We partner with prisons and branches of the local YMCA to gain access to these populations, who are notoriously hard to reach. More than 75 per cent of prisoners are unemployed on release, and it is eight times harder for someone with a criminal record to find work than for someone without one. Evidence suggests that if the transition to work has started before release, then the chances of finding and keeping a job – and, crucially, preventing re-offending – increase dramatically. Re-offending costs the UK £13 billion each year, and the estimated cost for every single re-offender is c£200,000 per annum. England and Wales release 90,000 prisoners per annum, and 60 per cent re-offend within two years. A steady job cuts the probability of re-offending by up to 50 per cent, the single intervention with the highest degree of success. The YMCA is the largest provider of safe, supported accommodation for young people in the UK, which includes everything from emergency accommodation through to supported longer-term housing and youth hostels. Their philosophy of supporting young people holistically means they provide not only a bed but also help a young person gain the training, skills and confidence to go on to lead independent lives.

In light of the above, *Harness the Horses* offers an opportunity to develop valuable skills before offenders are released from prison, or while people are transitioning out of homelessness. There are technical skills taught which are specific to agricultural and conservation work, but also foundational skills that are applicable to a wide range of jobs in the equestrian industry, which tend to offer positions with accommodation, away from problem peers. The participants also work towards a recognised qualification.

The British Horse Society (BHS) stage one will allow them to seek employment in any horse yard in the UK or abroad. For many participants, this will be their only professional qualification. Equally important, the programme has numerous positive effects on self-belief, engagement, self-esteem and a sense of accountability, all of which are very important for survival and success in the outside world. Very often we hear participants comment that it is being with the horses that makes them feel like human beings.

While not exclusively, the programme has focused in particular on unemployed, homeless or ex-offender women as one of the most vulnerable categories in society. More than 50 per cent of women prisoners report having experienced physical, emotional or sexual abuse. Self-injury in prison is appallingly high, as about a third of women self-harm while in prison - which is five times greater than for males. In addition, 80 per cent of women in prison have diagnosable mental health problems, four times greater than the comparable figure in the community.

Homelessness is also widespread and is both a symptom and cause of unemployment and substance abuse, with approximately 4 in 10 women prisoners leaving prison without accommodation. The YMCA groups that attend also consists of many women who sought emergency accommodation as a result of domestic violence.

The aims of the programme are to help conserve Richmond Park using traditional methods, which is the element that provides purpose. This is actual conservation work that would not get delivered without the help of the programme participants. This is a core element – it is not training, or for the sake of it, it is real work that makes a considerable contribution to society. It also highlights the way we are connected to nature, it helps participants explore their relationship with nature and the world around them. Sir David Attenborough, a Patron of the Friends of Richmond Park, leads a high profile campaign urging everyone to tread lightly in the park. We help deliver this through working with horses rather than heavy machinery. This endorsement is equally important. Our participants feel they are making a contribution to something worthwhile. We focus on offering the specific professional and practical skills, while also creating a context that is conducive to psychological well-being. It is a workplace with a lot of tolerance for frustration.

We developed a core curriculum based on British Horse Society and British Driving Society qualifications, and added additional elements about working with horses in agriculture and conservation. The 12 weeks allow for at least three different activities of the "farming year": harrowing, clearance and habitat creation. The 12-week programme consists of a daily routine involving care of horses including mucking out, grooming, maintenance of the equipment and harnessing the horses. The team then sets out to complete three or more hours of work in the nature reserve. The work includes harrowing, clearing bivouacs, habitat creation and other conservation work. Alongside this practical work, there are mentoring and reflective sessions about being part of a team. Everyone rotates across all tasks.

Equine coaching is a vital part of the rehabilitation incorporated in *Harness the Horses*. As well as allowing the participants to reflect on the experiences of the week, it also helps them understand the relationships they are forming with the coaching team, the horses and each other. Sessions take place every week and last for around two hours. A number of different horses are used and are selected on what is perceived to be the next developmental need of the group. All sessions involve working as a group although there are opportunities for individual work within that context. Equine-assisted learning sessions demonstrate how social relationships work in a herd of horses. Observation and activity with the herd teaches cooperation and negotiation in a non-aggressive environment, where there is no punishment. It teaches about the different roles everyone plays in a group and that our behaviours are not fixed and can change – and that patience is important if you want to succeed. It offers a way of building negotiated relationships. It is in this setting that *Harness the Horses* participants first experience their new relationships. For many, it is a very different workplace and, of course, radically different to anything they have experienced before. Instead of authority being located in one person, everyone was encouraged to take their own authority while focusing on completing the tasks.

Struggles

The realities of this programme mean it is not always smooth sailing. Initially, the pressures from their very complex lives outside meant that many participants just found it very hard to stick to the time boundaries that had been set. They would be late, they'd want to leave early or they wouldn't show up at all. We asked these questions: "Do you want it enough to be here at 7am? Are you prepared to experience discomfort in order to be here?"

There was no punitive element to the time boundary, but it was made clear that the horses are on a timetable where they need regular food intake. Feeding is a shared responsibility: to be integrated as a full member of our team we asked them to take part in the shared responsibilities. This gave them a level of shared authority in a role as well as a degree of responsibility. They couldn't pick and choose when to give the horses breakfast, for example, as they need to be regularly and consistently fed. We emphasised the importance of routine and showed them how the horses were happier once they had a routine. This functioned as a metaphor to show how we could all benefit from this. The moment we as individuals accept and respect structure, we can experience a higher level of contentedness and an absence of chaos. They experienced the pleasures of working in a structure which is nurturing: the camaraderie from having shared objectives, working as a team etc. as opposed to rallying against what they perceived as a negative structure (the discipline).

For some people, the disruptions of their home lives and the emotional reconnection they were experiencing were not things they were willing and/or ready to work with. As things became more "real" in the therapeutic work, timekeeping deteriorated for some participants. Some stopped coming. We inform participants that we all need to make some decisions about commitment and laid out the terms. We were all there to work as a team, therefore individual attention choices were no longer feasible. The team depended on everyone keeping to what was agreed and it was important going forward that they committed to that. We acknowledged the difficulties they were facing, however the boundaries needed to be kept and respected. On the whole, this is the point in the programme when the working group emerges.

Diary studies

The diary study was added to ensure a subjective voice for all participants. As a longitudinal device, it also allowed us to track changes in observations throughout the programme. For example, initial entries were very concrete and more school-like ("correct" responses). From week three, however, diaries became much more evaluative.

A central theme was how participants managed to connect to emotions, and experiencing and being aware of emotions is a core theme that surfaces time and time again. Gerry wrote,

> I am starting to look after myself and the way I am around people and horses. I feel they can pick up on how I am feeling. It's nice to work in a team and have good people around me.

This observation demonstrates that they picked up quite quickly that they are talking about building relationships with the horses. Their own behaviour affects the horses' behavior, and vice versa. "I realise that I have to be a lot calmer but firm with horses," said Manjeeta.

It wasn't just the horses. The work itself helped heighten awareness of emotions. As Aisha put it: "We were quickly realising that clearing bivouacs was good to release some anger – I learned to turn my anger into effort, which felt really good."

Managing anxiety was one of the first tasks that was tackled in the coaching sessions. Aisha describes how, in one coaching session, she reacted when the horses galloped towards her: "When they ran towards us I should have stood my ground rather than run and get scared - if that happens again that is what I shall do."

This learning took place quite quickly. "I am starting to feel a lot more confident driving the horses. I am also starting to enjoy it," said Mangeeta in week five. "I know my confidence is growing each day with the horses."

Thoughts even turn to the future: "I was thinking I could quite easily go out to a job and do a lot of manual work as I enjoy it and like seeing a result in the jobs I do," states Chen.

What seemed to make the transition between fear and confidence was trust, Chen wrote in her diary:

> It was lovely to feel that the horses trusted us so much. There was a little hesitation when trying to get horses to canter as they were in a corner of the paddock, but we succeeded in the end which felt great.

One of the core assumptions of the programme is that meaningful and purposeful work in a cooperative environment will have a positive effect on psychological well-being and self-belief. The survey results already indicated this, but here are the women in their own words: "I like to work in a team. I enjoy seeing what work I have achieved. I like being out in the open. Fresh air, horses, cart I'm very lucky to have this opportunity," said Chen.

Mangeeta comments on achievement and care for others:

> I felt I had achieved something good. It was nice to work out in the park. I love to work outside with nature. The horses worked extremely hard and it was nice to bring them back and give them a good clean.

That the work was purposeful came through clearly also: "The park has lots of different environments (habitats) for all sorts of animals and knowing we have helped make these feels good," said Frankie. Giles concurs: "It was hard work on the fences in the area (bashing the posts in) but well worth it. It helps the natural environment."

The process of learning is a process of internalisation, of incorporating felt experience into the inner world of fantasy and reason. We have encouraged each participant to take their own authority to use the training programme by examining, and trying to understand, the parts they play in the dynamics of the group and wider system. This was the main purpose of the equine-assisted coaching sessions. Below are some reflections on the learning that took place beyond the horsemanship.

"It felt nice to learn something new and experience something new. I also didn't expect to be hands on so soon. So that was a positive thing because I enjoyed it", reflects Zac. Initial anxieties and trepidation of "the new" made way for enjoyment. We talked about self-sabotage a lot. The tendency not to participate because you're too scared you won't be able to do it, or you'll make a fool of yourself manifested itself strongly in the beginning of the programme. Being "hands-on" tackled that head-on!

Miranda described her learning about anxiety another way: "I need to work on my lack of confidence and self-doubting: people are not always thinking what I think they are thinking." This learning is also echoed by

Lucy: "I learnt that we need to communicate more with each other. Just because the horse has a harness on doesn't mean that you're in control."

Case studies

Due to the high levels of prescription medication that some of the participants were on (e.g. Subutex and Methadone), their tasks had to be restricted to yard duties. We helped those participants build relationships with the horses, which resulted in several different positive outcomes:

1. Perspective taking
2. Putting the needs of others first
3. Reconnecting with emotions

For example, Sharon talked about how her one positive childhood memory was being with her mother and a horse. Working with the horses not only helped her reconnect with that feeling; it also revealed to her that the difficult childhood she had been referring to perhaps hadn't been as bad as she had thought. Therapeutically, this was a valuable first step towards allowing her to tolerate an ambiguous world rather than one that has been split into good or bad.

Case study: Natalie

My head is like a washing machine going round and round and round… but when I'm with the horses it's empty – quiet even. I feel at peace with myself and can concentrate on the task. It's a nice feeling to be away from the madness of prison and even from my own thoughts for a few hours. I've got more out of this experience than I thought I ever would.

Natalie was very articulate and driven and really wanted to turn her life around. Natalie was convicted of manslaughter because the jury could not decide whether it was her partner or herself who had smothered their baby. She had been suicidal on multiple occasions when she first entered the prison system. Self-harm in women's prisons is an unfortunately common issue. Natalie was eager to work with the horses and took to the curriculum well. She very soon established herself as a solid team member; she was diligent, dedicated and hard working. Therapeutically, Natalie found it quite difficult to engage and to open up. We talked about the very limited opportunities in prison to address the emotional issues around her crime (Natalie had been offered one session with a forensic psychologist in the near two years since she had been incarcerated); we also talked about whether it may be useful to explore those issues. We focused on generic issues around self-esteem and self-efficacy, so Natalie didn't feel pressurised into making disclosures or into working at an emotional level she wasn't ready for. Natalie was with us over a period of eight weeks in which she learnt about horses and horsemanship; towards the end of her time with us, she started missing some days and then one day she stopped coming.

At the Holly Lodge Centre in Richmond Park we share the space with an education centre that has children in attendance; on one occasion Natalie got upset when a group of children came in. She told us the children were the same age as her son would have been now. For the first time, she started talking about the key thing that she was struggling with.

Case study: Donald

"I believe if I put as much effort as I put into getting my heroine into my recovery then my recovery will be a lot easier to overcome." Donald has mild learning difficulties; whether these are congenital or caused by prolonged and severe drug use is unknown but nevertheless, his cognitive ability is impaired. We had to adapt the curriculum substantially and keep everything very simple. For example, he had difficulty remembering the names of certain food stuffs and of common tools. We adapted the programme to account for his very limited reading and writing skills and very much focused on building relationships.

Donald was one of the few people who wanted to talk in his cohort; and he would talk, and talk at length. He would talk so much that the whole group would get angry with him. The content of what he was saying was very nearly always the same: how he was struggling with relationships from the past, how he felt unloved and how he didn't get what he needed when he was a child. While Donald could articulate his feelings, he was also very disconnected to them. He had all the right psychological language but found it very hard to connect to it emotionally. Anger was one of the first issues that came to the fore in the sessions with the horses, and observing two horses fighting in the herd allowed him a connection to his own anger. It was a very powerful moment.

Donald attended the programme diligently. We kept the pace right down because he found learning challenging. We spent more time focusing on the relationship with the horses and looking at very tangible ways in which he could feel useful and have a purpose; getting praise was important for him and he would ask for it constantly. Donald was very unfit when he first came and found the working environment quite alien. We introduced him to rules and regulations, boundaries, the importance of a predictable routine and of looking after horses' needs first. This induction into the world of work allowed for a lot of useful conversations in the therapeutic space: the importance of structure, of predictability, depending on someone and being depended on by someone and of being accountable and having a clear role within the wider context.

The thread running through the different themes was the anxiety of his imminent transition to life outside the prison walls and being able to return to work for Operation Centaur. We agreed to be in touch in six months and allowed the option that he could contact and visit us at any time he felt like it. At the end of the engagement we had someone who could take perspective and could connect in relationships. He had experienced an environment in which he could trust and more importantly he had also managed to start moving away from an either-or way of being in the world.

Case study: Alex

"Today was the first time in a long while that someone trusted me. It was an emotional but positive experience." Alex was achingly shy, found it hard to work in a group and had an ASD and ADHD diagnosis. She was also terrified of horses, but as we worked with her, her self-esteem and confidence grew noticeably. The cleaning out of the hoofs had struck her the most during the *Centaur Inside* process. This is one of the exercises we ask them to do where we bring in a farrier who explains the complete trust required from the horse when cleaning out their hooves. They also explain that horses are flight animals and the most important thing they have is their legs as they allow them to run away from predators as fast as they can. For Alex, the initial fear of "Am I going to get kicked by cleaning these hooves?" changing into "Maybe this horse is scared of ME and whether I'm going to hurt HIM!" struck a very powerful chord. Harming and being harmed is a central tenet in Alex's life. Alex is in prison, convicted of an armed robbery charge. She wanted six cans of cider, had no money, and decided that the best thing to do was to point a pellet gun at the owner of an off-licence before walking out. During her time in prison, she has been a prolific self-harmer mainly through swallowing items such as tooth brushes and TV aerials. As already pointed out, self-harming in female prisons is a big issue. We are always acutely aware of this with anyone, because self-harm is a potential recourse when people are going through transitional periods in their life. Because of Alex's openness to the programme, I agreed to meet with her and her case worker several times after *Centaur Inside* ended. During this period it transpired that Alex found it challenging to identify her gender in a binary way and was drawn to having a gender reassignment. Importantly, through her case worker, Alex has sought contact sporadically over the last year and has wanted reassurances that there was going to be a place for him on the programme. (Alex has from this point asked to be referred to as a he). Operation Centaur is a great place for Alex to try out his new gender identity in a supportive, non-threatening working environment.

Questionnaires

The participants are asked to complete a series of questionnaires during the course of the 12-week programme – once before they start the programme, once during week 7 and once 2 weeks after the programme has finished. The data collected is analysed to assess behavioural change. In particular, after the programme, we want the participants to: be more likely to take the initiative; exhibit more effort at work; be more persistent; have higher self-efficacy; be more engaged; have higher self-esteem; have a lower locus of control.

Self-efficacy refers to an individual's belief in their own ability to achieve things successfully. It reflects confidence in your ability to control your own motivation, behaviour, and social environment. For validity reasons, we used two measures of self-efficacy: the General Self-Efficacy Scale (GSES) and the Schwarzer and Jerusalem Self-Efficacy Scale. The General Self-Efficacy Scale (GSES) consists of 17 items representing the three aspects underlying the scale: initiative, or the lack thereof – willingness to initiate behaviour; effort – willingness to expend effort in completing the behaviour; persistence –persistence in the face of adversity. Participants were asked to indicate whether various statements applied to them (strongly disagree, disagree, no disagreement/agreement, agree, strongly agree; range 1–5). Results indicate that participants were twice as likely to take initiatives following the programme than before. This is in line with expectations.

The second measure of self-efficacy, the Schwarzer and Jerusalem Scale, is a 10-item psychometric scale. It is designed to assess optimistic self-beliefs to cope with a variety of difficult demands in life. In contrast to other scales that were designed to assess self-efficacy, this one explicitly refers to personal agency, i.e., believing that your actions can lead to successful results. This scale therefore not only validates the GSES but also Rotter's Locus of Control measure below.

Engagement was measured using the Society of Human Resource Management Engagement Scale, a standardised scale used globally although not specifically with prison populations. This survey consists of 10 items and is the most used measure of engagement. Employee engagement is an important driver of organisational success. When employees are engaged with their work, they're more fulfilled, more productive and more motivated. Since many workplaces now use this measure, we felt it important to include it in this programme. It can also stand as a proxy for concepts such as commitment, motivation and job satisfaction. This shows that engagement increased steadily throughout the project, with a 17 per cent increase over the 12 weeks. This is in line with expectations.

Self-esteem is how we value ourselves; how we perceive our value to the world; and how valuable we think we are to others. Self-esteem affects our trust in others, our relationships, and our work. Positive self-esteem gives us the strength and flexibility to take charge of our lives and grow from our mistakes without fear of rejection. A person with low self-esteem feels unworthy, incapable and incompetent. Some signs of low self-esteem are a negative view of life; perfectionist attitudes; mistrusting others – even those who show signs of affection; blaming behaviour; fear of taking risks; feelings of being unloved and unlovable; dependence – letting others make decisions; fear of being ridiculed. The Rosenberg Self-Esteem Scale (RSES) is a self-esteem measure widely used in social science research. It consists of ten items answered on a four-point scale – from strongly agree to strongly disagree. Five of the items have positively worded statements and five have negatively worded ones. The scale measures self-esteem by asking the respondents to reflect on their current feelings. The Rosenberg self-esteem scale is considered a reliable and valid quantitative tool for self-esteem assessment. Participants reported increased self-esteem of nearly 60 per cent. This is in line with expectations.

Who is responsible for things happening in the world? As the environment around you changes, you can either attribute success and failure to things you have control over, or to forces outside your influence. The orientation someone chooses is called locus of control and this has a bearing on their long-term success. Locus of control describes the degree to which individuals perceive that things happen as a result of their own behaviour, or due to forces that are external to themselves. People who develop an internal locus of control believe that they are responsible for their own success. Those with an external locus of control believe that external forces, like luck, determine what happens.

Research has shown that the more internal the locus of control is the more likely you are to settle successfully in to normal life. The Rotter External–Internal Locus of Control Scale is a 23-item scale to assess whether a person has a tendency to think situations and events are under their own control or under the control of external influences. This scale is a forced choice paradigm in which a person chooses between an internal or external interpretation.

Participants' level of locus of control lowered marginally midway through the programme, but had a 38 per cent drop by the end. This indicates that the women were more likely to attribute the causality of what happened to themselves rather than to external agents or events. This finding was in line with expectations.

In order to attribute these longitudinal changes to the intervention rather than to chance, we also collected measurements from a control group. Participants who took part in *Harness the Horses* took four times as much initiative; put 40 per cent more effort into work; were four times more persistent; were five times more engaged; were eight times more confident in their own value; shifted locus of control to internal, whereas controls almost stayed static; and, overall, the participants were five times more likely to believe in their ability to get things done.

Ultimately, by teaching these participants horsemanship they learned about themselves and their place in the world. *Harness the Horses* delivered skilled, confident, qualified professionals, who are more prepared to face the difficulties of life. We have also made *Harness the Horses* available to the general public in the form of taster days, where everyone can come and experience the amazing horse–human relationship through working together. We are particularly heartened that participants from many years ago still turn to us, and in particular our horses, to come back to when they are facing a life crisis. The value of a safe space in one's life is not to be underestimated, yet is so often taken for granted.

The Centaur Club

Simon came to us rather panicked. On his way to us he got lost, and arrived 45 minutes late. We reassured him and he calmed down somewhat. He didn't want to talk – although he did devour a plate of cake and biscuits. Eventually he joined the group and made a start.

From his first encounter with horses, Simon was convinced they "hated" him. He would smile and whenever he was asked anything, he would say he "felt depressed", "hated being here", "wasn't good at anything". He was determined to be separate, but nevertheless kept looking and close to the action.

Over the course of the day, we learned that Simon's negative appraisal didn't actually mean anything negative at all. When I asked him to help wash the horse with me, he initially refused. When I re-casted my request to ask him "can you just hold this", he became very engaged in the task. It didn't take long before others were involved in the task and I could stop facilitating.

People diagnosed with ASD are usually regarded as struggling with social communication, interaction and imagination. Work with Simon illustrates that understanding his worldview doesn't take huge leaps. With a few small interventions, he became a fully integrated member of the group. By engaging the group in a task that was new to all, a shared understanding of the work was mutually created – and inclusive.

Caring for horses is hard work. In "The art of stress" (Bicknell and Liefooghe, 2006) I talk about the Foucauldian notion of souci-de-soi, the care of the self, as a continual artistic endeavour that is never finished or fixed. In psychiatric assessment, care of the self physically is one of the first indicators of mental health stability. Care is central to *The Centaur Club*. This programme brings together children and young people who are in foster care, and who are finding the experience challenging. Through working with horses, we teach them what care is all about – for themselves, and for others.

The Centaur Club is a space where young people can experience being with horses and others, and thereby learn about their own place in that world. The key aim of *The Centaur Club* is to undertake meaningful work with a purpose, where everyone can participate regardless of age and ability. The fact that the activities do have a wider impact is an important part of the philosophy behind *The Centaur Club*. Helping others and the environment is a great way to help yourself, too. In this respect, horses are incredible teachers.

The Centaur Club offers an opportunity to engage in meaningful tasks that make a positive impact on the natural environment. It allows participants to be part of a healthy and fair work and learning environment, improve their psychological well-being, and offers a therapeutic intervention to hard-to-reach groups. Most of the participants in *The Centaur Club* have been children or young adults in foster care. Taking care of horses is therefore particularly poignant. To date, some 200 participants have benefitted from the programme.

As we have seen in the previous chapter, work gives us a purpose, and working with horses to deliver important conservation work is exciting. Using Shire horses is a sustainable way to manage parkland. Not only are they are offering a much-loved service to London's landscapes, the figures stack up and it makes sense both environmentally and economically. In addition to helping conservation work, we also help preserve traditional methods which are an important part of Britain's cultural heritage. The skills of working the land with horses are disappearing fast. To be part of a team of working horses is an impressive experience. We developed a core curriculum based on British Horse Society qualifications, and added additional elements about working with horses in agriculture and conservation.

Equine-assisted learning sessions demonstrate how social relationships work in a herd of horses. Observation and activity with the herd teaches cooperation and negotiation in a non-aggressive environment, where there is no punishment. It teaches about the different roles everyone plays in a group and that our behaviours are not fixed and can change – and that patience is important if you want to succeed. It offers a way of building negotiated relationships.

It is in this setting that our club members first experience their new relationships. For many, it is a very different space and, of course, radically different to their usual environment. Instead of authority being located in one person, everyone is encouraged to take their own authority while focusing on completing the tasks. This leads to accountability, an awareness of being part of a larger unit, and eventually to contentedness in a safe environment.

When Raquel started at The Centaur Club she was very timid, both around the horses and in her interactions with both the volunteers and other young people. She appeared to lack confidence both physically and socially. Raquel was quiet in the group, and found it hard to speak out. Raquel was interested in forming a relationship with the horses from the outset and one of her first questions was how she might foster a horse. Her natural care and empathy with the animals has helped to her participate in activities around the horses' care which require her to be physically robust, and to work with others to accomplish the tasks. We have seen Raquel grow hugely in physical confidence. She appears to now enjoy being the tallest and strongest member of the group, and takes pride in helping a younger member with the heavier or more cumbersome tasks such as filling and carrying hay nets or pushing a wheelbarrow.

Raquel has had to invest something of herself physically in order to learn how to groom and look after a pony, and in doing so build a relationship. She has learnt how to put on a head collar and to tie up her pony using the correct knots and become more confident and dextrous with physical tasks. She has also learnt to groom the horses, and to name the various brushes. Grooming a horse is a very physical task and at times a dirty job, something

Raquel found difficult at the start. However, she has developed an under-standing of how important it is to care for the horse, even if it means getting a bit dirty and this has helped her to engage with the activity. In the Equine Assisted Learning Sessions Raquel has participated in challenges which re-quire her to give directions to other group members and volunteers. The work takes place in a large outdoor sand arena and Raquel has had to learn to really shout to make her instructions heard. She has started to find her voice, and realise she can make herself heard. This has hugely improved her confidence as she learns to take charge and work as part of a team.

When other members of the group give the instructions, and Raquel's task is follow their directions whilst leading her pony we have noticed she naturally rewards the horse with pats or a stroke after every task. The con-cept of care is ever present with Raquel as she is mindful to look after the horse's mental as well as physical state; she is equally extremely careful in the way she grooms and brushes her pony. Raquel has brought her camera in so she can take photos to document all her hard work and seems proud of what she has achieved.

On day one, Alexa proudly told us about her Russian background, and her love of Russian horses. Horses quickly became a proxy for her mother, so she was able to channel at times difficult emotions through the work with the horses. Throughout the programme, she worked closely with Raquel. Even though she was the younger of the pair, she took the initiative most of the time. She would particularly shine during the equine coaching sessions. She was comfortable with leading the horses immediately, and took great care to follow instructions correctly. When the exercises became freer, she expressed herself in a confident manner. Even when things became a strug-gle, Alexa would persevere, and undertook many initiatives and creative decisions. In the art sessions following the horse work, she showed herself to be innovative and increasingly confident.

Jolly and happy on each occasion, Christa was the life and soul of the group whenever she was there. From the beginning, it was clear that she had some boundary issues. She would stand really close to the people she was talking with; she was greedy when it came to sharing food; and wanted to be first whenever an activity was suggested. She also claimed to be "bored" and "tired" very soon on those initial sessions. Gradually, however, her be-haviour adapted. Through observation of the herd in the field, we showed how important it was for the horses to have space between them. Penny Black, the lead mare, clearly showed that when she went very close to the other horses, the horses would give way. We interpreted this to Christa that getting too close might lead to others walking away. Equally, we used the horses to illustrate the importance of turn taking, and of sharing food. Horses helped Christa to see that perspective taking was important.

Antoinette initially presented as a frail looking girl, very thin, who looked cold but refused to wear more clothing. Her braces made her feel less confident than some of the others. She struck up a friendship with Penny Black, an eight-year-old mare who is also the alpha in charge of the herd. Quietly, Antoinette participated in the exercises with Penny Black, grooming her, and delighting in preparing her food. We managed the ending carefully, as it was clear that Antoinette was leaving a dear friend in Penny Black. We assured her she would be well looked after, and encouraged her to visit.

The senior of the girls, Amy was initially rather shy. She really felt the pressure of examinations, and at first seemed distracted. She was unsure about being taller than the others, and oscillated between wanting to help look after younger participants, or sticking by herself. A turning point for Amy was the day she happened to be the only person attending the after-noon session. Everyone else was away for Easter, and she started somewhat forlorn. However, on her own we could give her 1-2-1 time and this really got her to open up and embrace the challenges of looking after horses. She was absolutely thriving, and emphasised to us how important it was for her to do things with a purpose. She told us about her affinity with the horses, with the park, and with conservation. She couldn't thank us enough that day. A week later, Amy brought her friends – she asked us if they could stay. We told her she was welcome to show them around and introduce them to the horses, but they couldn't stay for the actual work, although we were happy for them to wait in the park. Amy was clearly proud of the environment she worked in, and wanted to share this with her friends. She was feeling really special.

In the accounts above, we have demonstrated that participants were likely to take more initiatives as the programme progressed. Indeed, some were very creative. As time progressed, there was real commitment, and all exhib-ited continued effort at sometimes repetitive tasks. We have hundreds of these vignettes, and collectively they give a sound body of evidence for *The Centaur Club* intervention. We believe that the care and coaching combined engaged all participants, and engendered a sense of pride, and therefore self- esteem. While the environmental work was limited due to the range of ages, there was nevertheless a sense of doing activities with purpose, and with care. Anecdo-tal evidence from carers suggests that even at home, changes were in evidence. Social workers have also commented on how they hadn't seen some children in such an animated and social state before – very promising feedback.

Centaur Connections

In the past few decades, many challenges around differences in organisations have been successfully addressed with regard to gender, race, age, sexual-ity or disability. Indeed, legal frameworks exist to protect discrimination at work of any kind, including during the recruitment process. Yet against this backdrop, there is still one large stigma remaining – that of mental health at work. The Royal College of Psychiatrists (2015) believes that stigma is one of the greatest challenges facing people with mental health issues, and those with a mental health diagnosis who are workless are doubly stigmatised. This is because work is both central to identity and to the way an individual is perceived by others. Also, it is only through work that the great majority can achieve a level of financial status that permits full participation in society.

We have experience of working with one particular subgroup, those diagnosed with autistic spectrum disorder (ASD). According to the National Autistic Society there are about 332,600 people of working age in the UK with an autism spectrum disorder (ASD). Only 15 per cent of adults with autism are in full-time employment; only 9 per cent are in part-time employments. According to the TUC, 61 per cent of those out of work say they want to work, while 79 per cent of those on Incapacity Benefit say they want to work. More than half (53 per cent) of adults with autism said they want help to find work, but only 10 per cent are getting the support.

Mainly, the problem is to do with different attitudes towards the diagnosis. One of the dominant ways of viewing disability, the medical model, presents the impairment as the cause of disabled people's disadvantage and exclusion. If an employer decides that a person cannot work for the company because of their diagnosis on the autistic spectrum, rather than considering how to make the workplace suitable for an autistic person to work in, that employer is probably being influenced by the medical model of disability.

There are other ways of looking at this, however. The social model identifies attitudes which may impede disabled people's participation and equality. There is prejudice and ignorance surrounding autism and mental health. There are also workplace practices, procedures, cultures, unwritten rules and communication forms which do not take account of people who either have a mental health diagnosis or are non-neurotypical. It is here that *Centaur Connections* can make a real and valuable difference. If we can change the opinion of the gatekeepers into the organisation, we may be able to convince them to make adjustments and create appropriate job opportunities. The big shift in opinion needs to be from a deficit model (what is wrong) to an enabling model (there are differences here that can give us an advantage).

Centaur Connections is an equine-assisted learning programme designed to overcome stigma and to address some of the difficulties in understanding others who are different. We aim to bring together people diagnosed with ASD and neurotypical HR recruitment specialists to learn to work together and explore their differences. According to the Royal College of Psychiatrists report, it is at the recruitment stage that the stigma functions at its most powerful, hence our choice of this particular organisational group. If we can convince this group, then a big hurdle to employment has been overcome.

Creating workplaces which welcome neurodiversity and mental health diversity requires us to move out of our comfort zone. It's easy being around people who are socially adept and confident; it's more challenging interacting with someone who is socially awkward and doesn't adhere to social norms. Most of us are scared of what we don't know – it's therefore easier to appoint someone who is neurotypical than someone diagnosed on the autistic spectrum. And it is this fear, this unfamiliarity, that we seek to redress. After all, I hope by now that we have demonstrated that we know how to make the strange familiar, and the familiar strange.

Throughout this book, I have argued that there is no more powerful learning than experiential learning. And nothing allows you to truly know another than entering a working relationship with them. Our sessions consist of small groups of matched people with a mental health diagnosis and recruiters, who are being taught to work with heavy horses over a very short (and busy!) period of time. We hope that by the end of the programme, perceptions about autism will be challenged – and some useful tips on employability will be gained. Ultimately, a workplace that is more mental health diverse is one that recognises neurological diversity, and is therefore a workplace that is better for all workers.

Often, people diagnosed with ASD have difficulty relating to other human beings, and would not accept closeness with another – but they will with horses. There's a bond that develops that is profound and natural. Our programme utilises this bond to create change. This involves establishing a presence with the horse and gradually nurturing the relationship. Horses don't do labels, they react to the energy you bring. And whether you are on the spectrum or neurotypical, they will no doubt teach you a lot about yourself, and about others.

Based on the principles of cooperative group work, we bring small mixed groups of ASD and neurotypical people together in a new environment and start teaching them a new set of skills: horsemanship. The core reason for the choice of skills is that it is (a) non-verbal and (b) relational. From our prior research with young people with ASD, we hypothesise that they will react in creatively different ways than neurotypical people, with the latter bringing a more classic task focus to the table. The learning mediated through the relationship with the horse forms the basis of exploring similarities and differences.

The steps of the programme, then, are to match senior recruiters, HR directors and recruitment consultants with people who are diagnosed with a mental health issue or non-neurotypical and are looking for work. We bring them together in a strange environment where they have to work together to learn new tasks jointly. As they learn the tasks, they learn about themselves – and about each other.

The hypothesis is for recruiters to have an increased understanding and awareness of people with mental health diagnoses and those who are non-neurotypical, thus minimising the stigma. We also convince recruiters it is worthwhile to make some adaptations for people with differences as they enter the workforce. For people diagnosed with mental health diagnoses and who are non-neurotypical, we facilitate the experience of the rigour of a traditional task focused approach, and provide learning about the world of work in a safe environment. Ultimately, this can lead to some real job opportunities, which is the aim of all our programmes described here.

Figure 8 Al Muhalhal (Abraxas Halimaar x Hadaya Meketaten) Zoltan, meeting Andreas for the first time, September 2005, Home Park, Hampton Court Palace.

Chapter 8

The whole horse

A coda

As Derrida (1976) points out in *Of Grammatology*, the beginning is always written when the story is already known. And when we use language to tell our story we cannot expect it to mean only what we want it to mean, because it has a semantic life of its own, and its meanings escape from us. I hope therefore that this gives everyone permission to take as much or as little from these writings as you wish. In concluding the story, I wanted to turn to a more autobiographical genre to allow this text a con-text. As a reflexive researcher, I decided that a coda was a better space to reflect.

The gift of kings

> "HRH, without prejudice, is sending you a stallion and mare, to be delivered by HM's air transport on Sunday".

This was the email that arguably set the whole Operation Centaur project in motion. In 2005, and somewhat out of the blue, I was notified that through the intervention of my friend HRH Princess Bazza bin Saud Abdulaziz al-Saud, her uncle had secured two horses from HM King Abdullah bin Abdulaziz al-Saud's stables for Operation Centaur. King Abdullah states that "for centuries our people have considered our horses to be one of our greatest treasures", and true to his word and the spirit of his countrymen and as a lifelong horse enthusiast, he has steadfastly supported the establishment and development of all equestrian pursuits within the Kingdom.

The Arab horse is famous throughout the world and is closely associated with the history of Riyadh as the breed was first developed almost 3,500 years ago by nomadic tribes of the Najd Plateau. Pure, desert-bred Arabian horses, whose lineage can be traced back to that Najd dynasty are a rarity whose many qualities are revered by the Bedouin: loyalty, beauty, endurance, intelligence, speed and courage in battle. Traditionally Arab royals and tribal leaders have strived to collect and breed the best Arabian horses and HM King Abdullah is no exception having collected and bred Arabian horses since his youth at Janadria farm.

Receiving horses from a king is, other than exceedingly generous, incredibly symbolic. Further symbolism came from the markings of the horses that had been chosen.

> When Allah went to create the horse he spoke to the South Wind and said: "I want to create an animal out of you. Make yourself dense." And the South Wind did, and from this dust Allah created a kamayt-coloured animal. "I create thee, O Arabian. I give you the chestnut color of the ant; Men shall follow thee wherever thou goest; thou shalt be as good for flight as for pursuit. To thy forelock, I bind victory in battle. Thou shalt be for Man a source of happiness and wealth; thy back shall be a seat of honour, and thy belly of riches; every grain of barley given thee shall purchase indulgence for the sinner".
>
> Then Allah blessed the horse and gave him the sign of glory and happiness - a white star on his forehead.
>
> (from a Bedouin legend)

Of the markings on a horse's face, a star was considered the most lucky, followed by a stripe or blaze that reached down to the lip, which meant his master would always have milk. The stallion whom we named Zoltan (Sultan, the King) has all the above characteristics: chestnut, star and blaze down his lip, resembling the trickling of milk. *Fajr al-Taniyah*, translated as *Dawn of the Second Coming*, was the desert-bred grey mare that accompanied Zoltan, who tragically died by impaling herself.

Finding a voice

I am writing this overlooking the Mediterranean just north of Tel Aviv in a space made available to me, with characteristic graciousness, by my great friend Dr Susan Kahn. As a child, I always did my homework on the kitchen table, despite many a desk being available, which is also where I gravitated to here. There is something about being at the heart of things, being held and nurtured. Kitchen tables on the whole are *gemütliche* spaces.

The week before I arrived had been tough. My old canine friend Klaus had to be put down at the grand old age of 13. Not bad for a German Shepherd, yet that length of companionship leaves a gaping hole when it is no longer there. Staff changes take time to settle in. A close friend is splitting up with his girlfriend. Endings and loss are everywhere.

As I walked through Ben Gurion Airport on Holocaust Memorial Day, I'm reminded of the importance of safe spaces. I imagine what it must feel like to be Jewish and to return to a homeland following the holocaust horrors. The Middle East may seem a strange place to write, with its instability and conflict, but it feels convivial. And creative and productive.

It's never either/or. The symmetry of the Arabian horses and the Israeli writing space play in my mind. As London-based Israeli chef Ottolenghi (2012) points out, hummus may succeed where politics fail. I reflect that in a much smaller way, the therapeutic frames we provide are safe spaces, too. The context reminds me of the work I have been focusing on most of my life, the phenomenologies, dialectics and discourses of relationships. The self and the other, vulnerability and demand, victim and perpetrator, coach and coachee, patient and therapist.

This book is some fifteen years in the making. I'm finally writing it.

The whole horse

I connected with horses early on in life, when a chestnut mare called Cora caught my attention. She lived in a field not far from my house, and whenever we were driving anywhere I would insist we make a detour via this field. This initial obsession later translated into actual riding, competing and teaching. During this time, even though I had my own horses, one old riding school horse specifically springs to mind. His name was Goliath, and I recall whenever I felt sad, I would sit silently on the straw bed in his stable. He would come over, put his head down, and sigh. I never had to be convinced that it was possible to have strong emotional connections with horses. It was there from the very beginning. That stable was the only place I felt safe and understood.

I reconnected with horses after a decade absent from them. Living in London combined with studying was not conducive for equine company. When I did reconnect, they again shaped the direction of my life. I teamed up with Edward MacDowell, who has persistently over half a century succeeded in keeping horses working on the streets of London. Jointly we set up Hampton Court Shires, dedicated to keep working horses relevant in urban settings, mainly through heritage and conservation work.

So horses made me move away from Central London to the West, Hampton Court. This move heralded a move in career interest also. When I first thought I could make a contribution to this field, as a "good" social scientist I of course tried to reject the hypothesis of bringing my experience with horses and my training in psychology and psychotherapy together. Why should this work? Why not enjoy my horses and be as good a therapist, scholar and teacher as I can be? A lot of my reading on the subject had divided me. On the one hand there was the spiritual melting-pot idea, on the other the more rigorous but far less colourful approach. I visited programmes and went to experiential days all over the world.

In Bangkok, where I have been a visiting professor for nearly twenty years, my friend and colleague Siriyupa Roongrerngsuke indulged me in my wish to brave the Thai jungle to discuss the human–animal relationship with the abbot of Wat Pa Luangta Bua Yannasampanno, better known as the tiger temple, which helped me form some early ideas about de-centring. It was a memorable trip. Also in Thailand, my friend Pasin Bua-on found the last remaining island where villagers harvest coconuts with the help of monkeys, and duly came to translate the conversations I wanted to have with them.

The working relationship with animals fascinates me, and I learned a great deal talking to falcon handlers in Dubai, where these majestic birds soar in urban canyons created by skyscrapers in pursuit of pigeons. Again, one person's fancy is another's vermin.

On a trip to Germany I met a remarkable woman who would give direction to my quest. StarrLee Heady "Star" was a pioneer by birth and by nature, being a second-generation settler in Colorado. She is no-nonsense and works with some of the toughest crowds a therapist can imagine – navy seals who have experienced theatres of war in Iraq and Afghanistan. I joined her in Florida for training and qualified with her in the Eagala model. Another influential figure in shaping my views on equine-assisted psychotherapy was Troy Kuntz. An old-school American cowboy, we spent a brief but intense five days in Chicago working with a herd of horses at an Eagala advanced training seminar. Both Star and Troy inspired me to pursue the idea and set up the Operation Centaur programme.

The final word

These final words I write in Barcelona, looking eastwards across the Mediterranean towards Tel Aviv. Over a decade of data collection, hundreds of participants, thousands of hours on horseback, in the sand school or in the field later, this book is finally done. Throughout writing this book, I have reflected and learned copious amounts. In particular about the significance of the horses' role in the therapy. Traditional talking therapies need to adapt if they are to remain relevant. These days, people use the language of therapy and have lost the meaning, the connection with what is beyond language – what is real. Horses facilitate a powerful connection with ourselves, and with others. It just never ceases to amaze me.

There are many people to thank on this journey. Dr Lucia Berdondini has been my supervisor throughout my professional life. The feeling of certainty you experience when you truly believe that someone is always going to call your blindspot, regardless of how devastating that might be, is priceless. Andrew Moody, Raul Aparici and Holly Emberton all helped in bringing this manuscript into being. James McKie has coached me to greater physical fitness to complete the task, and is helping me develop exciting new therapeutic projects. The privileged spaces of Historic Royal Parks and Palaces where we conduct our work, and the people who manage them, have fostered this work greatly. None of this could have been achieved without the many donors, participants, corporations and organisations who have placed their trust in Operation Centaur.

Finally, my home team. Edward MacDowell and Tom Nixon, ably assisted by a team of staff and volunteers, keep our herd of horses content – a healthy, happy, working herd, without whom none of this would be possible, and from whom wisdom is just there for the taking.

References

Benjamin, J. (1998). *Shadow of the Other: Intersubjectivity and Gender in Psychoanalysis.* Abingdon: Routledge.

Berdondini, L. (1999). Bullies, victims, bystanders: how do they react during anti-bullying sessions?, unpublished PhD thesis.

Berdondini, L. and Liefooghe, A.P.D (2005) Beyond "bullies" and "victims": a systematic approach to tackling school bullying. In: L. Greenwood, L. (ed.), *Violent Adolescents: Understanding the Destructive Impulse.* London: Karnac.

Berdondini, L. and Smith, P.K. (1996) Cohesion and power in the families of children involved in bully/victim problems at school: An Italian replication. *Journal of Family Therapy* 18, 99:–102.

Berget, B., Ekeberg, Ø. and Braastad, B.O. (2008). Animal-assisted therapy with farm animals for persons with psychiatric disorders: Effect on self-efficacy, coping ability and quality of life, a randomized controlled trial. *Clinical Practice in Epidemiology and Mental Health* 4(9). Online at: https://www.ncbi.nlm.nih.gov/pmc/articles/PMC2323374/

Bettelheim, B. (1967). *The Empty Fortress: Infantile Autism and the Birth of the Self.* New York: Free Press.

Bick, E., 1964. Notes on infant observation in psycho-analytic training. *The International journal of psycho-analysis*, 45: 558–566.

Bicknell, M. and Liefooghe, A. (2006) The art of stress. *Journal of Organizational and Occupational Psychology* 79(3): 377–394.

Bion, W.R. (1961). *Experiences in Groups and Other Papers.* London: Tavistock.

Bion, W.R. (1965). *Transformations.* London: Karnac.

Bion, W.R. (1967). Notes on memory and desire. *Psycho-analytic Forum* 2(3): 271–280.

Bion, W.R. (1970). *Attention and Interpretation.* London: Tavistock.

Bradshaw, J. (2011). *In Defence of Dogs: Why Dogs Need our Understanding.* London: Allen Lane.

Buber Martin, (1947). *Between Man and Man.* London: Routledge.

Burgon, H. (2003). Case studies of adults receiving horse-riding therapy. *Anthrozoös* 16(3): 263–276.

Carroll, L. (1949). *Alice's Adventures in Wonderland and Through the Looking Glass.* London: Harper Press.

Derrida, J. and Spivak, G.C. (Trans.) (1976). *Of Grammatology.* Baltimore: Johns Hopkins University Press.

Eagala. Equine Assisted Growth and Learning Association. Online at: http://www. eagala.org

Erikson, E.H. (1974). *Dimensions of a New Identity*. New York: W.W. Norton & Company.

Evans, D. (1996). *An Introductory Dictionary of Lacanian Psychoanalysis*. Routledge.

Foucault, M. (1963). *The Birth of the Clinic*. Paris: Presses Universitaires de France.

Foucault, M. (1975). *Discipline and Punish*. Paris: Gallimard.

Freud, S. (1895). *Studies On Hysteria*. London: Hogarth Press.

Freud, S. (1900). *The Interpretation of Dreams*. London: Hogarth Press.

Freud, S. (1905c). *Jokes and Their Relation to the Unconscious*. London: Hogarth Press.

Freud, S. (1913). *On Beginning the Treatment*. London: Hogarth Press.

Freud, S. (1923). *The Ego and the Id*. London: Hogarth Press.

Freud, S. (1930). *Civilization and Its Discontents*. London: Hogarth Press.

Gabriel Y. (2015). Identity, choice and consumer freedom – the new opiates? A psychoanalytic interrogation. *Marketing Theory* 15(1): 25–30.

Gallup, G.G., Jr. (1970). Chimpanzees: self-recognition. *Science* 167: 86–87.

Grandin, T. (1995). *Thinking in Pictures*. New York: Doubleday.

Grandin, T. (2002). Do animals and people with autism have true consciousness? *Evolution and Cognition* 8: 241–248.

Grant, A.M. (2011). Is it time to REGROW the GROW model? Issues related to teaching coaching session structures. *The Coaching Psychologist* 7(2): 118–126.

Hacking, I. (1990). *The Taming of Chance*. Cambridge: Cambridge University Press.

Heimann, P. (1950). On counter-transference. *The International Journal of Psychoanalysis* 31: 81–84.

Higashida, N. (2013). *The Reason I Jump: The Inner Voice of a Thirteen-year-old Boy with Autism*. New York: Random House.

Hinshelwood, R.D. and Skogstad, W. (2002). *Observing Organisations: Anxiety, Defence and Culture in Health Care*. Abingdon: Routledge.

Horse Whisperer, The (1998). Film, Redford, R. (dir.), USA: Touchstone Pictures.

HRH The Prince of Wales, in: Stewart, P. (2017). *The Last Herd: The Story of London's Last Working Shire Herd, in the Royal Parks and Historic Royal Palaces*. London: Photography into ART.

Kahn S. (2017). *Death and the City: On Loss, Mourning, and Melancholia at Work*. London: Karnac.

Kelekna, P. (2009). *The Horse in Human History*. Cambridge: Cambridge University Press.

Klontz, B., Bivens, A., Leinart, D. and Klontz, T. (2007) The effectiveness of equine assisted experiential therapy: Results of an open clinical trial. *Society and Animals* 15: 257–267.

Kohanov, L. (2001). *The Tao of Equus: A Woman's Journey of Healing and Transformation Through the Way of the Horse*. Novato, CA: New World Library.

Kohanov, L. (2003). *Riding Between the Worlds: Expanding our Potential Through the Way of the Horse*. Novato, CA: New World Library.

Kohanov, L. (2011). A tribute to Tabula Rasa. Online at: https://eponaquest. com/a-tribute-to-tabula-rasa/

Lacan, J. (1949). The mirror stage, source of the i-function, as shown by psychoanalytic experience. In: Fink, B. (trans.) *Écrits*. New York: W.W. Norton & Company.

Lacan, J. (1956). Sur les rapports entre la mythologie et le ritual expose, *Bulletin de la Societe francaise de Philosophie* XLVIII: 113–119.

Lawrence, W.G. (1979). *Exploring Individual and Organizational Boundaries: A Tavistock open systems approach*. London: Karnac.

Liefooghe, A.P.D. (2001). Bullying at work, unpublished PhD thesis.

Liefooghe, A.P.D. and Mackenzie Davey, K. (2001). Accounts of workplace bullying: the role of the organization, *European Journal of Work and Organizational Psychology* 10(4): 375–392.

Liefooghe, A.P.D and MacKenzie Davey, K. (2010). The language and organization of bullying at work. *Administrative Theory and Praxis* 32(1): 71–95.

Lyotard, F. (1979). *La condition postmoderne: rapport sur le savoir*. Paris: Les Éditions de Minuit.

Miller, P.H. (2002). *Theories of Developmental Psychology*. Basingstoke: Macmillan.

Monty Roberts: The Real Horse Whisperer (1997). Film, Thomas, M. (dir.), USA: RIDICULOUS Pictures.

Müller, F.M. (2000). *Upanishads*. Ware: Wordsworth Editions.

Obholzer, A. and Roberts, V.Z. (1994). *The Unconscious at Work: Individual and Organizational Stress in the Human Sciences*. Abingdon: Routledge.

Ogden, T.H. (1997). Reverie and interpretation. *Psychoanalytic Quarterly* 66: 567–595.

Olsen, S. (2003). *Horses Through Time*. Roberts Rinehart.

Ottolenghi, Y. (2012). *Jerusalem*. Ebury Press.

Perls, F. (1969). *Gestalt Therapy Verbatim*. Lafayette, CA: Real People.

Plato, Cooper, J.M. and Hutchinson, D.S. (Trans.) (1997). *Complete Works*. Indianapolis, IN: Hackett Publishing.

Queen, The: A Passion for Horses (2013). Leese, I. (dir.), UK: BBC.

Raulff, U. (2017). *Farewell to the Horse: The Final Century of Our Relationship*. London: Allen Lane.

Rashid, M. (2000). *Horses Never Lie: The Heart of Passive Leadership*. Rexburg, ID: Spring Creek Press.

Rice-Edwards, M. (2017). Understanding the Art of Riding, DVD, Ham House Stables. Online at: www.hamhousestables.com/dvd/

Rigby, K. and Slee, P.T. (1993). The Peer Relations Questionnaire (PRQ) Adelaide: University of South Australia.

Roberts, M. (1997) *The Man Who Listens to Horses: The Story of a Real-life Horse Whisperer*. Random House.

Ross, J.M. (1999). Once more onto the couch: Consciousness and preconscious defenses in psychoanalysis. *Journal of the American Psychoanalytic Association* 47(1): 91–111.

Royal College of Psychiatrists, The (2015). *Stigmatisation of People with Mental Illness*. The Royal College of Psychiatrists.

Rudolph, C. (2015). *The Art of Facilitation, with 28 Equine Assisted Activities*. Tehachapi, CA: Rising Moon Ranch.

Rustin, M. (2006). Infant observation research: What have we learned so far? *Infant Observation* 9(1): 35–52.

Rycroft, C. (1995). *A Critical Dictionary of Psychoanalysis*. London: Penguin.

Sandler, C. (2011). *Executive Coaching: A Psychodynamic Approach*. New York: McGraw-Hill Education.

Sarti, M.G. and Cossidente, A. (1984). Therapy in psychosomatic dermatology. *Clinics in Dermatology* 2(4): 255–273.

Schultz, P., Remick-Barlow, A. and Robbins, L. (2007). Equine assisted psychotherapy: A mental health promotion/intervention modality for children who have experienced intra family violence. *Health and Social Care in the Community* 15(3): 265–271.

Spinelli, E. (2008). Coaching and therapy: Similarities and divergences. *International Coaching Psychology Review* 3(3): 241–249.

Stapley, L.F. (2003). Developing trust: obstacles and understanding. In: J. B. Kidd (ed.), *Trust and Anti-trust in Asian Business Alliances.* London: Palgrave.

Stapley, L.F. (2006). *Individuals, Groups, and Organizations Beneath the Surface.* Abingdon: Routledge.

Tennyson, A. (1842). *Poems.* London: Moxon.

Trotter, W. (1916). *Instincts of the Herd in Peace and War.* Basingstoke: Macmillan.

Waddell, G., and Burton, A.K. (2006). *Is Work Good for Your Health and Wellbeing?* London: The Stationery Office.

Wells, T. (2016). The Shireshank redemption: storm as women lags get horses for 'therapy'. *The Sun.*

Western, S. (2012). *Coaching and Mentoring: A Critical Text.* Thousand Oaks, CA: SAGE Publications.

White, S. (2013). *An Introduction to the Psychodynamics of Workplace Bullying.* London: Karnac.

Winnicott, D.W. (1949). Hate in the counter-transference. *International Journal of Psycho-Analysis* 30: 69–74.

Winnicott, D.W. (1951). Transitional objects and transitional phenomena: A study of the first not-me possession. *International Journal of Psycho-Analysis* 34: 89–97.

Winnicott, D.W. (1957). *The Child and the Family.* London: Tavistock.

Winnicott, D.W. (1971). *Playing and Reality.* London: Tavistock.

Winnicott, D.W. (1973). *The Child, The Family, and the Outside World.* London: Penguin.

Xenophon and Morgan, M.H. (2006). *The Art of Horsemanship.* Mineola, NY: Dover.

Zugich, M., Klontz, T. and Leinart, D. (2002). The miracle of equine therapy. *Counselor Magazine* 3 (6): 22–27.

Index

horsepower 11, 26
The Horse Whisperer 14
Hunt, R. 14

interconnectivity: corporate culture
82–6; external and internal 79–82; in
nature 77–8; recovery therapy 86–91;
see also connection

Kahn, S. 62, 63, 128
Kazakhs 12
Kelekna, P. 11
Klontz, B. 31, 32
knowledge 23, 60; self-knowledge 28, 45,
55, 62; and transference 31
Kohanov, L. 22–3, 54, 67
Kuntz, T. 130

Lacan, J. 60, 80
language 11, 13, 26–7; de-centring 30,
53, 70–5, 82–6, 102; of "Equus" 14;
the talking cure 27
Lawrence, W.G. 49
leadership 9, 63; and authority
103–4; avoiding language 74, 82–6;
in dysfunctional groups 35; and
fitting in 102; and followership 100,
101; horses' 23, 25; and managing
relationships 102–5
Liefooghe, A.P.D. 94, 97, 120
London Transport Museum 26
Lyotard, F. 18

MacDowell, E. 129
Mackenzie Davey, K. 94
marking the horses 128
Menzies, I. 96
Miller, P.H. 62
Mobius strip 80, 82
movement, creating 32, 40, 41, 99–101;
corporate coaching 65, 66, 82; and
interconnectivity 78, 82, 89
Müller, F.M. 13

naming horses 5, 55
Napoleon, Emperor 15
National Ban Bullying Day 94
natural method 14–15

Obholzer, A. 49
objectification 48–9

observation 60–2, 97, 112, 121, 122;
and anthropomorphism 66–8, 95;
de-centring the human 68–70, 74–5;
from a distance 85, 93; and meeting
the other 65–6; psychoanalytic 62–3;
and self-recognition 63–5
obstacles: building 55–7; moving
through 74
Oedipus 62
Ogden, T.H. 33, 68
Olsen, S. 12
Operation Centaur 15, *24*, 40–1, 72,
98, 116, 117, 127; connections and
reconnections 39–40; and the Eagala
model 37–8; evaluation model
5; exercises 40–1; movement and
direction 40; Prince of Wales's praise
9; programmes 2–4; psychoanalytic
approach 19; safety 38–9
organisations 19, 20, 41; and bullying
94–5; challenging discrimination
123–4; de-centring language 3, 74,
82–6; relating to otherness 65, 66
otherness: de-centring the human
68–70; and interconnection 78–81, 89;
meeting the other 65–6; observation,
and self-recognition 63–5; projection,
and anthropomorphism 66–8; and
self-esteem 118; and togetherness 56
Ottolenghi, Y. 128

Parelli Program 14
Perls, F. 47
Plato *(Phaedrus)* 29
positivism 28
prisoner rehabilitation 3, *42*, 43–4; and
anthropomorphism 66–7; building
obstacles 55; connecting to emotions
110–11, 115–17; horses as a method
45–6; learning about addiction
52–3; space boundaries 49–51; time
boundaries 51–2; transition to work
110–11, 115–18; vulnerability 48
projection 34, 53, 61, 97; and
anthropomorphism 66–8; and
transference 32, 34
psychoanalysis 17, 19, 20; and
knowledge 23; methods 46–53; and
observation 62–3; the "self" 28–30

Rashid, M. 25
Raulff, U. 11, 13